LINCOLN CHRISTIAN UNIVERSITY

P9-DEO-046

Smart Parenting During and After Divorce

❖

PETER J. FAVARO, Ph.D.

New York Chicago San Francisco Lisbon London Madrid Mexico City
Milan New Delhi San Juan Seoul Singapore Sydney Toronto

The _McGraw·Hill_ Companies

Library of Congress Cataloging-in-Publication Data

Favaro, Peter J.
   Smart parenting during and after divorce / Peter J. Favaro. — 1st ed.
      p.   cm.
   ISBN-13: 978-0-07-159755-5 (alk. paper)
   ISBN-10: 0-07-159755-7 (alk. paper)
   1. Divorced parents—Attitudes.   2. Divorced parents—Family
relationships.   3. Children of divorced parents—Psychology.   4. Divorce—
Psychological aspects.   5. Child rearing.   6. Parenting.   7. Parent and
child.   I. Title.

   HQ759.915.F38   2009
   306.89—dc22   2008034455

Copyright © 2009 by Peter J. Favaro. All rights reserved. Printed in the United States of America. Except as permitted under the United States Copyright Act of 1976, no part of this publication may be reproduced or distributed in any form or by any means, or stored in a database or retrieval system, without the prior written permission of the publisher.

1 2 3 4 5 6 7 8 9 10 11 12 13 14 15 16 17 18 19   FGR/FGR   0 9 8

ISBN 978-0-07-159755-5
MHID   0-07-159755-7

McGraw-Hill books are available at special quantity discounts to use as premiums and sales promotions or for use in corporate training programs. To contact a representative, please visit the Contact Us pages at www.mhprofessional.com.

This book is printed on acid-free paper.

This book is dedicated to the memory of my

loving parents, Peter and Josephine.

983

121738

Contents

Part 3

Co-Parenting Successfully

Part 4

Divorced Parenting for Ages and Stages

Part 5

Making Visitation Schedules Work

Part 6

Dealing with Common Problems

Part 7

Special Concerns and Crisis Situations

Part 8

Moving On

Preface

THIS BOOK IS the product of my more than two decades of experience helping to educate divorced and divorcing parents, most of whom have come to me through the New York Unified Court System.

I have been a court-appointed expert, custody evaluator, mediator, and therapist in more than six thousand cases over the past twenty-two years. In that time I have developed hundreds of practical strategies to help divorced and single parents deal with the universal problems encountered when sharing and managing custody of children.

Some of the information I present is common sense, but it's not the kind of thinking that comes naturally to people embroiled in highly emotional conflict. Of all the behavior that I have observed in working with families going through divorce, I have been most struck by the confusion and sadness a poor co-parenting relationship can bring to a child. I want to help you avoid that.

Parents who don't want to spend all of their time and money going to court can find nonadversarial methods for resolving custody and visitation conflicts. You and your co-parent can be successful in raising your child to become a happy and productive member of society.

This book contains helpful information, strategies, and resources on visitation, communication, conflict resolution, anger management, scheduling of holidays and visitation, decision making, the effects of divorce on children at different ages, the influence of a parent's social life on children, negotiating under both good and bad circumstances, and much more.

The information is arranged by topic so that you can quickly find help relevant to your particular situation. This book is written in plain, no-nonsense language, without fluff or psychobabble.

The book also includes over a hundred tips or "takeaways"—bite-sized pieces of advice that I hope will make you and your child enjoy each other and the time you spend together a lot more!

Life during and after divorce doesn't have to be as difficult as we sometimes make it. I'd like the chance to show you that you can make your co-parenting relationship work for the sake of your child.

Part 1

Understanding *Your* Conflict

Topic 1
Smart Parenting During and After Divorce

MOST PARENTS KNOW that the quality of their relationship with one another during and after the divorce process will influence the psychological adjustment of their children—but often they forget it.

I ask every set of parents who come to see me the same set of questions. First, I ask whether they are sure that they love their children and would do anything to ensure that they grow up healthy and well. Predictably, both say, "Of course."

Then I ask, "What if that meant donating some of your blood to keep them well?" Predictably, both say, "Yes."

I follow by asking, "What if they needed your bone marrow? That procedure can be very painful, you know." Predictably, again, the answer is yes, so I continue.

"All right, that's all well and good, but what if they needed one of your kidneys? A doctor might tell you that this is a dangerous operation and that if things go wrong on the operating table you might perish so your child could live." My somber tone is not enough to dissuade parents from quickly reporting that they would make the trade if they were asked to—except for one poor gentleman who looked at me rather sadly and reported, "I might have to think about this more than most people would. I only have one kidney!"

Even after most confidently report that they would make the ultimate sacrifice for their children, I tell them I am not convinced. If both are so certain that they would donate blood, bone marrow, or a kidney, or even trade their own lives so that their children could have a happy, healthy life, why would they not sit in a room and have a civilized conversation about their children, knowing full well that their failure to do so will hurt their children?

Often, this dialogue helps people to think differently about the nature of their petty disagreements with one another. I am hoping it might do the same for you.

Smart parenting is all about trading the momentary relief of venting anger and frustration at your co-parent for the benefit of raising healthier, more productive, and less stressed children. The side effects of this trade include peace for you and an immunity to at least some forms of aggravation that might be created by your co-parent.

So, when you are tempted to opt for the quick relief, always ask yourself, "Is this worth hurting my kid over?" If the answer to this question is "no," you have become a smarter parent already!

Topic 2
The Common Threads of Conflict

Quick Tip: Don't lecture the co-parent. Give him an opportunity to respond. Then listen.

ALL CONFLICT OPERATES in the same way, whether it occurs between two individuals or between societies with oppositional ideologies. That is why when I lecture about conflict and conflict management, I start by outlining conflict's common threads or themes.

The common threads of conflict are (1) an increased sensitivity to criticism and insult and (2) intensity and direction. If you know how intense the conflict is (mild to severe) and what direction the conflict is heading (whether it is getting more severe, or *escalating*, or getting milder, or *de-escalating*), you can generally predict how the conflict will end.

Increased Sensitivity to Criticism and Insult

Conflict cannot exist without insult, as fire cannot exist without air. Generally speaking, people are not motivated to listen to people who insult them, and if they *are* listening, it is only to hear the criticism so they can formulate a counterattack.

Civilized communication is the exception rather than the rule when people are fighting over their children, so much of the conversation between high-conflict parents is insulting. Sometimes these insults are specifically intended to wound; sometimes even well-intended statements are perceived as insulting simply because the co-parents expect hostility from one another; or, worse, sometimes co-parents are insulting without even thinking about it.

High-Conflict Conversation

Here is an example of a typical conversation between two high-conflict parents.

> **Co-parent A:** Are you picking Joey up at the regular time tomorrow?
>
> **Co-parent B:** Of course. Isn't that what I always do on Thursday nights?
>
> **Co-parent A:** Except when you are working late, or stuck in traffic, or taking your girlfriend to buy shoes.
>
> **Co-parent B:** Huh?
>
> **Co-parent A:** Nothing.
>
> **Co-parent B:** What's with you? Why do you take every conversation I have with you to a nasty place?
>
> **Co-parent A:** I didn't say anything nasty. If you take it that way, you take it that way.
>
> **Co-parent B:** OK, I take it that way.
>
> **Co-parent A:** I'll see you tomorrow, then.
>
> **Co-parent B:** Make sure he's ready when I get there.
>
> **Co-parent A:** The king has spoken.

Low-Conflict Alternative

The entire interaction could have been trimmed down to:

> **Co-parent A:** Are you picking up Joey at the regular time tomorrow?
>
> **Co-parent B:** Sure thing. I will be there at 6:30 P.M.

The insulting part of the conversation was kicked off by the question *Isn't that what I always do on Thursday nights?* This is the first piece of advice that I give to co-parents to help tone down the conflict level: *Do not ask questions that aren't essential to the topic at hand.* When situations are tense, asking questions, especially pointed ones, is often seen as threatening. When threat increases, people tend to become insulted, and when they are insulted, barriers to effective communication go up quickly.

How to Limit Criticism and De-Escalate Conflict

You can put yourself in a better frame of mind to de-escalate conflict by adopting the following principles.

- Less is more.
- Stay silent when you are not sure that saying anything will do you any good.
- Don't add fuel to fire.
- Don't look to get the last word.
- Don't give your co-parent any opportunity to argue.

All of these tips are meant to control the level of conflict between you and your co-parent and limit the number of insults between you. The fewer insults there are, the more smoothly talk regarding your child or children will proceed. Remember, it takes two people to argue.

> **Q**uick Tip: Keep your mouth shut until the co-parent finishes talking. Nothing escalates an argument more quickly than one person cutting the other person off.

That is your first two-minute lesson in de-escalating conflict between you and your co-parent—and it's an important one. By "two-minute lesson," I mean it takes two minutes to *teach*. The amount of time it takes for you to learn might be influenced by how much money you want to pay a lawyer to help communicate what you can't communicate without the insults—and there is no guarantee that your lawyer will communicate without the insults. Some people pay a premium for that!

The Intensity and Direction of Conflict

Now, let's take a look at the second ingredient in the recipe for conflict. Conflict has an intensity and a direction. Conflict can either escalate or de-escalate. Further, it can rise to a boil quickly, or it can simmer to a boil over a long period of time. If you know where conflict is going and how fast it is going there, it is easy to predict the outcome.

De-Escalating Conflict

When conflict de-escalates, it means that things are simmering down, understanding is being reached, and you and your co-parent are becoming less sensitive to insult. These are all good things. This usually happens because you and your co-parent find a reason to do something positive for one another, or you simply grow tired of aggravation. When conflict de-escalates, the outcomes are

- Win-win
- Win-compromise
- Compromise-win
- Compromise-compromise

It might look as if win-compromise is listed twice, but it isn't. Remember, we are looking at both sides of the conflict, so it is listed as "win-compromise" and "compromise-win" to show that either side might compromise a little of what they want for the sake of reducing and ending the conflict.

Escalating Conflict

When conflict grows or escalates, by the time it reaches its boiling point (whether it does so quickly or over a long period of time) the outcomes are very different. They are:

- Win-lose
- Lose-win
- Lose-lose

When conflict escalates there is more for both people to lose, and by the end the conflict can be so draining that even a co-parent who "wins" still loses. To put it into terms that a lot of divorced parents in conflict can understand: if you lose your home, your savings, and your sanity in a divorce that could have been settled through civilized conversation, then even if you "win," you still have lost.

Let's take the example of a child whose parents are arguing over a vacation. Imagine that one of the parents has spent a lot of money paying for cruise tickets. In the excitement of booking the trip, this parent realizes that arrival time back from vacation will cause her to be a few hours late returning the child. So the parent's attorney sends the other parent's attorney a letter advising that the drop-off will be about two hours later than normal. The response is a refusal to permit this. The reason given is that the late drop-off would require the children to go to bed past their usual bedtime, creating needless stress on them. This kind of petty argument can create tens of thousands of dollars in cost and many days of aggravation—and if you find it difficult to believe that these are the kinds of issues parents in conflict engage over, think again. The result of this conflict is almost always stress on the children; escalating conflicts eventually trickle down to negatively influence their quality of life.

In the worst of divorce conflicts, the outcomes of escalation can be described as:

- Win-destroy
- Destroy-win
- Destroy-destroy

And of these outcomes, when the divorce process becomes particularly petty, hostile, and disagreeable, the most likely outcome is destroy-

destroy. People's lives can be shattered by a high-conflict divorce, and the greatest harm comes to the children.

If you get nothing else out of this book, I hope you get the importance of avoiding the insults and criticisms that escalate conflict. It's pretty easy to employ sarcasm, backtalk, and veiled threats, and to harp on the co-parent's idiosyncrasies and general outlook on life. After all, you likely know your co-parent well enough to know where a hit hurts the most. Restraint, therefore, is the order of the day. It might be helpful to imagine that whenever you throw a verbal punch at your co-parent, it glances off him and lands on your kids, too.

All too often, you might find yourself wanting to zing the other co-parent, or to get the last word, or to not be made a fool. But the underlying issue just might be resentment of the change and the tumult that often accompanies it. It's very easy to explain to yourself and others why life is miserable when you can convincingly prove that someone is making you that way. But the hardest part of the end of your relationship might be facing the prospect of moving on to the next phase of life—the part where you can no longer lean on the assertion that you aren't where you should be because of someone else.

As you will see by reading this book, your kids benefit when you can orient yourself toward *managing* your conflicts with the co-parent rather than winning them.

Topic 3
Assessing Your Level of Conflict

THERE ARE COOPERATIVE co-parents, there are high-conflict co-parents, and there are gradients in between; however, I would not say there are very many gradients in between. Everyone can tolerate a few communication problems, visitation mix-ups, and grumpy or fickle moods.

Most separated or divorced parents I have dealt with can manage small to medium conflicts with success. The co-parents who have problems with one another have anger and hatred left over from the marriage or relationship that are brought into decision making regarding the children.

Frequently, the angry co-parents think along these lines:

> She was a lousy spouse [partner], so therefore she is a bad co-parent. Bad people do not make good parents, so anything I do to interfere with her relationship with my child is justifiable. After all, why should I let my child be influenced by a bad co-parent?

With this line of thought, co-parenting problems occur because one parent is always trying to seek what the other parent is trying to prevent—a relationship with the children. When both parents feel this way, there is usually an all-out war over who should control the children's lives. These are the worst cases.

The more conflict there is in a co-parenting relationship, the more likely it is that parents are struggling with leftover issues from the relationship that may have nothing to do with the children at all.

Strategies to Reduce Conflict

When co-parenting conflict is high, certain strategies can help minimize the stresses and strains that ultimately filter down to the children.

Reducing that conflict is easier said than done, because it involves a number of behaviors that high-conflict co-parents are not willing to do. These behaviors include the following:

- Trying to trust your co-parent, who has shown himself to be untrustworthy in your eyes
- Giving kindness to and doing favors for your co-parent, who might not do the same in return
- Resisting the urge to seek revenge for wrongs that have been done to you

There is a kind of scorekeeping that goes on between co-parents who do not get along. This tallying extends to issues such as how many articles of clothing are at each parent's house to how many minutes of visitation need to be made up when one or the other parent is late. Notions of what is "fair" or "unfair" reflect what one parent gets for investment of money, time, or devotion to the children. In reality, what is fair to a parent with respect to minutes, or pairs of socks purchased, or dollars handed over in child support, or dollars owed but not received in child support, has little to do with the emotional health and welfare of a child, no matter how much you or your co-parent insist it does.

> **Q**uick **Tip:** Giving in on little issues isn't giving in—it's being smart enough to avoid a major confrontation that will earn you more aggravation and a possible trip to court later.

What matters to your children is growing up without having to make excuses for why their parents hate each other. What matters even more is that no child should feel forced to take sides in a conflict that they did not create.

You might disagree with all of this and argue that the effort your co-parent makes to either pay child support or demand more child support than is deserved goes to the emotional health of the child. Of course it does, but on a relative scale it is overshadowed by what your child learns from seeing the two of you present a role model of hatred, disgust, disdain, disrespect, and intolerance toward one another.

For the purpose of this book you are either low conflict or high conflict. If any of what I've just described applies to you, you are high conflict. If you cannot make a decision with your co-parent without court intervention, you are high conflict. If you must rely on your attorney to communicate the simplest of your child's needs and requirements to your co-parent, you are high conflict.

High-conflict divorce hurts children socially, emotionally, academically, and physically. Now that you know that, I hope you'll do all you can to prevent it—read on to find out how.

Topic 4
The Art of Avoiding War: How to De-Escalate Conflict

THERE IS AN art to being able to influence a volatile situation so that it moves back to the point of civilized discussion. Not every conflict can be influenced this way, though. So what do you do when someone is determined to pick a fight and no amount of careful communication can de-escalate it?

Negotiating custody and visitation is not like negotiating the sale of a business. In the sale of a business, the buyer and the seller did not fall in love with each other, get married, and have children together. The buyer of a business probably didn't have his heart broken by the seller. The point is, there are many emotional issues that go on in family and matrimonial cases. Some family conflicts have a long history with many chapters. This brings into the negotiation additional co-parent agendas that don't exist in business communication.

Some co-parents are so interested in revenge, scorching the earth, or hurting the co-parent that regardless of how reasonable you are prepared to be, there will be no reasonable negotiation. In these cases, if you communicate a willingness to compromise you will be blamed for having something up your sleeve. If you look the wrong way, blink the wrong way, or walk the wrong way, you will be blamed for trying to start a fight. The negotiation table is seen as an environment to attack you with a laundry list of your past misbehaviors, each item ready to insert at any point in the conversation. I have been involved in situations where one party desperately wants to abandon the stress and strains of the legal process and consents to arrangements that are unfairly generous to the other party. The response typically is, *If that is what he is willing to give, I want more. Anything he would be willing to offer that easily is not enough.*

These are some of the things that are said and done around a negotiating table in the presence of attorneys. Often people try to negotiate for themselves, but negative statements and attitudes do not signify a willingness to reduce or end conflict; they signify rage.

If you find yourself encountering this type of anger and you are alone, without representation, and not in court, leave the situation as soon as possible. These are the types of situations that can explode past the point of verbal arguments and become physical confrontations. This is true if you are a woman being screamed at by a man, or a man being screamed at by a woman. There is no de-escalating conflict with a co-parent who wants to pick a fight.

Tips for De-Escalating Conflict

Many times, things get bad, but not bad enough to fall apart. These situations can move from tense and hostile to conciliatory, given the right influence and the right attitude. Here are some pointers for moving the conflict in a positive direction.

Schedule Meetings with a Definite Start and End Time

When you know you are going into a situation that will generate conflict and disagreement, it helps to focus on the fact that the meeting will have some type of end. Schedule your conflict resolution or your negotiation and settlement meeting for a finite period of time. This way you can remind yourself that at worst, your difficult interaction will end in an hour, two hours, or whatever time you choose. It might end only until the next meeting, but at least you can focus on some short-term relief.

Respond to Attacks with Neutral Statements

For instance, if during the process of trying to resolve a conflict your co-parent makes a sarcastic comment, you have a choice to respond with your own sarcastic comment, to point out the sarcasm and criticize the co-parent for it, or to acknowledge the co-parent's frustration and say that you are frustrated as well. Here are examples of all three situations.

Example 1:

Co-parent A: I would like to have the children on Thursday evenings so I may help them with their homework.

Co-parent B: Oh, really? When did you stop hanging out with your buddies after work to make yourself available to the children?

Co-parent A: I stopped hanging out with them after I realized the kids were being left with a sitter on Thursdays and failing all of their spelling tests while you were at your "I hate men" meetings.

Example 2:

Co-parent A: I would like to have the children on Thursday evenings so I may help them with their homework.

Co-parent B: Oh, really? When did you stop hanging out with your buddies after work to make yourself available to the children?

Co-parent A: You see this? You see what I have to deal with? She can't let it go. This is what I hear every time I make some effort to see my kids. Listen to me—I have a right to see my children, and a right to help them with their homework. If you feel the need to trash me every time I do that, what am I supposed to do? I want custody.

Example 3:

Co-parent A: I would like to have the children on Thursday evenings so I may help them with their homework.

Co-parent B: Oh, really? When did you stop hanging out with your buddies after work to make yourself available to the children?

> **Co-parent A:** You know, I do not really think I need to respond to that. We are both frustrated. I wish we could just straighten out whether I may see the kids on Thursday.

The first two conversations bring more stress into the argument; the third conversation puts the antagonistic co-parent in a very interesting dilemma. If Co-parent B continues the sarcasm, she identifies herself as unreasonable, rigid, and unfair. If Co-parent B opts out of that mode of behavior, she can at least be excused for making an insensitive comment because her co-parent is willing to acknowledge that she is frustrated. It is a win-win for Co-parent A because he is reasonable and doesn't engage in the same type of immature behavior as his co-parent. Co-parent A also provides a way out of dealing with the can of worms opened by Co-parent B. Co-parent A inevitably wins out as the good guy, whether the conversation stays on track or goes south.

Example 3 is another great application of the adage that you can indeed catch more flies with honey than with vinegar. There is another plus side to this. Sarcastic retorts require exhausting mental energy. The last kind of pressure you want to have to deal with is having to provide witty and incisive comebacks every time you are harassed. It is so much easier just to remain focused on the topic at hand and to keep saying things like, "I don't see how anything productive could come out of my responding to that." This statement actually *is* a response to the taunt, one that says, "I will not allow myself to stoop to the level of immature name-calling that my adversary cannot avoid." Saying that without really saying it is an elegant and graceful way of allowing someone who is behaving stupidly to set and fall into their own traps.

Be Prepared to Give and Receive

Whenever you ask for something, be prepared to offer something as well. Conflict escalates when one co-parent thinks she is doing all the giving while the other is doing all the asking. In the same way, when you get something you want, don't just go to the next item on the list.

Express your appreciation and ask whether there is anything else the other co-parent would like to bring up before you move on.

Avoid Backhanded Compliments

For instance, do not say something like, "I am happy that the kids will be spending so much time with the both of us. It would have been great if you had showed them this much attention when we were together." When you dish out enough of those, eventually you will get a reaction that affects other aspects of this or future negotiations.

If You Refuse to Fight, There Can Be No Fight

Quick Tip: If the co-parent asks questions or makes comments that should not be said in front of your child, say, "If this is important to you, we can talk about it in private."

Finally, the most practical principle of de-escalating conflict is quite simply that it takes two people to fight. If your co-parent is fighting and you remain calm, eventually your co-parent will identify how unreasonable he is being, and it will be easier for you to show how difficult it is to reason with him. I have never seen a parent criticized or punished by a judge for failing to engage in a fight. People can sometimes assume that if they are not defending themselves it is an acknowledgement that they have done something wrong. This is an incorrect assumption. People who refuse to engage in petty arguments are more likely to be perceived as mature and in better control of themselves.

Topic 5
Seek Neutral Input to Solve Problems

THERE ARE TIMES when the right idea can come out of the wrong mouth.

When co-parents discuss parenting schedules or the needs and requirements of their children, past problems and mistrust can cause either one to automatically veto perfectly good suggestions and ideas. On the other hand, if the same suggestion comes from someone both parties consider to be neutral, it might sound like the best idea in the world. There are people who specialize in mediating differences of opinion between co-parents. These individuals call themselves *divorce mediators, parenting coordinators, special masters,* or possibly other titles, depending on what part of the country you are in and what types of services are available.

Over the past ten years a lot of attention has been given to the profession of parenting coordination. These are family helpers who mediate, help people open lines of communication, and straighten out disagreements regarding court orders and stipulations made between parents. In some jurisdictions they are given a level of authority that permits them to make new decisions, just as a judge would. In other jurisdictions, the scope is not that wide because parenting coordination is still quite new. A great way to learn more about parenting coordination and how it is developing is to make yourself familiar with the Association of Family and Conciliation Courts at afccnet.org. You will find this and other resources at the back of this book.

Parenting coordinators and related professionals come from a wide variety of fields. Some are mental health professionals such as psychologists, social workers, and counselors. Some are lawyers. A great option would be to see professionals who work as a team that includes an attorney and a mental health professional.

There are many other people who can be just as effective when it comes to helping co-parents agree on what is best for the children. A mutually trusted family member or friend, a neutral attorney, or a clergy member can function as a sounding board for discussing the needs of the children with both parents present.

Do not agree to talking things out in front of someone you do not trust, or someone you think is going to be partial to your side of the issues. This can easily backfire. A mediator who fears she will not be seen as neutral may go out of her way to reinforce the other side of the story so that no one criticizes her for being partial. It is best to find someone who is neutral, who has no motivation to be partial, and, if possible, someone you know can make practical suggestions and craft fair compromises.

Try not to use anyone who has already listened to one side of the story, and instead try to schedule your first meeting at a time when both people can be present. The helper might want to listen to both people separately, but their stories won't be separated by too much time.

Always remember that a successful compromise gets you a little of what you want in some areas and encourages you to give up a little in other areas.

Topic 6
How to Negotiate with a Reasonable Co-Parent

NEGOTIATION IS A vitally important means of saving time, money, and aggravation when trying to figure out what is best for children—both in court and out of court. The less willing people are to negotiate, the more you will be surrounded by important (and often expensive) court-appointed professionals. Negotiation is an opportunity to reach common ground in an atmosphere that is more civilized and gentle than the combative and competitive arena of high-conflict litigation. In simple, practical terms, it never hurts to try to negotiate when it comes to the best interests of your children.

Here are some proven tips for successfully negotiating custody, visitation, and many other aspects of your family or matrimonial case. These points are presented in no particular order, but they are all important.

Know the Costs

Understand that when lawyers and courts are involved, there is a price on negotiating. It costs money to talk through a lawyer, schedule court dates, and so on. Even if you are being represented at no or low cost, indirect costs exist: lost pay for time off, babysitters or childcare, gas and other transportation expenses, and the overall value of your time. Finally, there is the cost to your body and mind that being involved in the stressful atmosphere of negotiations exacts. This can often be the greatest cost.

The flip side of this principle is that there is a benefit associated with closure, or the end of your negotiations. Proceedings have a beginning and an end, and when negotiations are prolonged because of arguments over insignificant details, there is a point of diminishing returns. Stop negotiating when most of the big line items are done. Do not stand on principle. If you choose to stand on principle, be prepared to pay a lot of money for the privilege. For instance, is it really worthwhile to pay lawyer fees of several thousand dollars to add thirty minutes to your side of the visitation schedule?

Stay Reasonable

The best way to help your co-parent be reasonable is by being reasonable yourself. This often translates into being a patient listener. A reasonable attitude can be communicated by restating the co-parent's position before giving your opinion on it. Refraining from exploding with comments like "That's robbery!" or "That is the most unreasonable position I have ever heard" is important. You can convey the exact same sentiment by saying, "I am thinking about what you are asking for, and I do not feel comfortable with it." There is tension and anxiety underneath even the most reasonable negotiations, and these emotions can turn a rational conversation into a free-for-all. When civilized conversation breaks down into a shouting match early on in any negotiation process, great damage is done to the process as a whole. That is because the negotiating parties will always be expecting the process to deteriorate back to that point. Another way of saying this is that there will be no trust. If you feel yourself becoming too tired or too tense to maintain a civil demeanor, take a break and rest.

Know What You Can Give

Never come to the negotiation table empty-handed. Be prepared to talk about what you are willing to give. People often make the mistake of going to a negotiation with no expectations and no idea of what is being negotiated. Their attitude is "I'll see what they are asking for and take it from there." This is an extremely poor strategy because it does not account for what would happen if *both* sides came into the negotiation with that mindset. Usually, this strategy results from laziness or from the belief that maybe the other side will ask for far less than you would have offered.

Don't Expect to Get Everything You Want

Never come into a negotiation expecting to get everything you want. This is a mistake that people make often when they are negotiating custody and visitation. One party decides they are offering "a great deal" or "the best deal" up front and assumes that "the deal will not get any better, so let's just agree and end this thing." Even if what is being offered is a good deal, the person considering it might not perceive it that way, but rather as evidence that one is trying to control or strong-arm the negotiations. There is something to be gained from the process of give-and-take that occurs on the way to a conclusion: you and your co-parent both feel as though you have participated in the bargaining.

Prioritize What You Want

Prioritize what you are bargaining for in terms of things you must have, prefer to have, and wish to have but could live without. It is helpful if you can deduce, decipher, or elicit those things from the other bargaining party as well. If you prioritize what you are bargaining for in this way, you can set goals for where you would like to be at the end of your negotiation. For instance, for some people a successful negotiation ends when they get 75 percent of everything they must have, 50 percent of what they prefer to have, and 30 percent of what they wish to have but could live without.

Prioritizing into these categories can provide a helpful image of what people are striving for and what the negotiation satisfies. They also form a common language for you and your lawyer to gauge your success or satisfaction at the end of a negotiation.

Do Not Ask for "One More Thing" at the Eleventh Hour

If you prioritize what you want ahead of time, you will not come up with "one more thing" just before the deal is closed. Just one more thing can kill all of the progress you have worked so hard for.

Turn the Small Yes into a Big Yes

Putting someone in an agreeable frame of mind sometimes requires negotiating small points with skill. Sometimes it is necessary to show people that saying "yes" will not kill or weaken them. Start with small points and work your way up when negotiations stall early in the process. Follow every yes with a question of what you might be able to offer in return.

Topic 7
How to Communicate with a Reasonable Co-Parent

PARENTS OFTEN SAY they cannot "communicate" with their co-parent. Reasonable communication is always possible as long as everyone's main goal is to communicate reasonably. This is often overlooked because parents forget the reason why co-parenting communication is important: it is the basis for solving problems concerning children.

Instead, parents get sidetracked into using communication about the children to hurt or punish the co-parent. Reasonable communication often produces reasonable communication, but when it is impossible you might want to go to page 34 and read about communicating with an unreasonable co-parent. This advice applies to parents who can communicate reasonably or who see that there is potential for reasonable communication.

In every communication there is a message and there is "noise." Think about trying to listen to a good song on a radio that has static or background noise behind it. Together, the message and the noise represents a "package" of communication. Effective co-parenting communications seek to make that package as effective as possible by increasing the quality of the "song" and decreasing the presence of the "noise."

Reasonable communication is:

- Direct and to the point
- Without barbs or surprises
- Respectful

Reasonable Versus Unreasonable Communication

The following communication is a great example of reasonable communication: "Can we please set aside some time so that you can give me some information on how our son is doing in school?" This is a direct communication. It asks a single question. It has an element of polite speech in it ("please"). It is considerate of the fact that the co-parent who is being asked for information might not be able to talk at that moment. It does not imply anything about the competence of the co-parent who has the information. It uses the respectful characterization "our son," so that no one's sense of belongingness regarding the child is threatened. It is an effective "package."

Now let's take the same subject of communication and wrap it in a very different package: "Your new job is obviously interfering with your ability to manage my son's schoolwork. He told me he failed a spelling test this week. Since you do not care whether I'm involved in this process I am going to have to get my lawyer to write a letter to the school so that I can have access to his grades."

This is a complicated and negative communication. It may seem that the main goal is to inquire about a child's schoolwork, but it is actually to harass the co-parent on the other end of the communication, express the belief that he is incompetent, and threaten future communication through lawyers.

How the "Package" Makes a Difference

There is communication, and there is the "package," or the way you deliver the communication. Whenever we push buttons in the co-parent we are communicating with, we lessen the chance that she will hear what we want to tell her because we are greasing up the communication with other agendas. When people are reasonable, they try to solve problems. In the second, hostile, communication just discussed, checking on the child's schoolwork seems to be the last thing on the communicator's agenda.

Reasonable communication requires that you concentrate on the topic and that you review what you are saying to make sure there are no barbs, thorns, or other pokers mixed into your message. Use elements of polite communication.

1. **Use polite terms like "please," "thank you," and "you're welcome."** These are lessons you learned when you were three years old. An added benefit of this habit is to provide a positive role model for your child.

2. **Be considerate when asking a time-sensitive question.** When a response is time sensitive, apologize for the pressure but specify a time when you need an answer. Here is an example:

> *My mother is coming in from out of town unexpectedly, and even though it is not my weekend I would like to know if it is possible to have Billy on Sunday for the day. I'm sorry this is short notice, but if you could let me know by tomorrow evening, I will have time to make some plans.*

3. **When the question is not time sensitive, suggest that your co-parent think about it and get back to you when she has an opportunity.** Obviously this is effective only when the other co-parent is responsible enough to remember to get back with an answer.

4. **Communicate effectively without making attacks.** This is definitely possible to do. Here is an example:

> *It has been difficult making arrangements for summer camp because you have not returned my last three phone calls or replied to my last note. Soon we will miss the deadlines for registration, which will create an even bigger problem. Summer camp is important, and I do not want to miss the deadline for registration. I would like to speak with you directly about it and would hate to have to settle this through attorneys. Please call me by the day after tomorrow so that we can straighten the issue out before it becomes a mess. Thank you.*

This letter is strong. It records the difficulties that have occurred in the past. It identifies the goal of not making the problem worse. It also notes that communicating through attorneys is objectionable but may be necessary as a last resort.

5. **Don't use barbs.** Avoid communications that start out reasonably but throw in a zinger at the end. Consider the following example.

> *Thank you for sending me the medical insurance cards I asked for last week. The name of Jamie's new pediatrician is Dr. Beller. His office number is 555-6545.*
>
> *By the way, when you send next week's check, could you include the $55 you have owed me for the last four months to cover the money I laid out for eyeglasses?*

The last paragraph is an example of a little zinger—not a big deal, mildly to moderately annoying if it is unexpected. A co-parent absolutely has the right to ask for money owed, but there might be ways of asking that are more effective. Compare that communication to this one:

> *I have two things I need to communicate to you in this letter. The first is to thank you for sending me the medical insurance cards I asked you for. The second is to ask if you could send along the $55 I laid out for Jamie's eyeglasses.*
>
> *Regarding the medical insurance cards, these make my life a lot easier, so thank you. If you would like to speak with Dr. Beller about Jamie, his number is 555-6545. I know that money is tight for everyone, but we did have an agreement about paying for the glasses, and I really need reimbursement for them. If you can't send a check right away, can we talk about when we can straighten this out? Thanks in advance.*

The second communication is more up-front and more persuasive. The goal in the first letter seems to be to shoot a dart at the receiver. The goal of the second letter is to solve the problem. In the second letter there is empathy shown for the fact that "money is tight." Some people might see this as giving the receiver of the letter an excuse to not pay. The fact of the matter is that for $55, you cannot go rushing into court. Success is more likely when you are polite, direct, and respectful.

Topic 8
How to Negotiate with a Jerk

I DO NOT have any magic potions or incantations to drive the bully out of your life. Nor do I have any tips on how to make the unreasonable co-parent more reasonable. The main goal of the advice here is to try to help you control the damage you do to yourself and your children when you are engaged in a problem-solving effort with a co-parent who pulls you into high-conflict communications.

First, are you sure the co-parent is as big a jerk as you think he is? Of course you are sure. You couldn't be more sure, right? You are emotionally involved, though, so you should look elsewhere for validation. Your friends and relatives do not necessarily count if they are the type who tell you everything you want to hear just to make you feel better. The reason for seeking outside validation is that once you are convinced that the co-parent you are dealing with is hopeless and unreasonable, you will probably stop trying to do all of the things that produce good results when people are reasonable (see the previous two Topics).

When you are certain that the co-parent is a genuine jerk and almost everyone who has an opinion agrees, there are certain facts you must accept.

True Facts About Jerks

You don't have to like these facts, but you do have to accept them.

- **Even the most reasonable, settlement-oriented professionals cannot control clients who are jerks.** Jerks do not listen to anyone, even their lawyers, because jerks know it all. That is part of what makes them, you know, the j-word.

- **Jerks will often get more than they deserve because they are stubborn.**
- **There is no guarantee that the jerk will get punished for her jerky behavior.** Sometimes jerks demand what is impractical but within their right to demand. In essence, jerks can't be punished for exercising their constitutional right to act like a jerk.
- **Jerks are entertained and amused by things non-jerks would like to avoid.** Jerks like to argue, and they enjoy being in a place where they can tell judges and anyone who will listen how victimized they are. They like to return to court whenever possible, even if it is a waste of money, just because they know it bothers you.

Practical Tips for Negotiating with a Jerk

In practical terms, when forced to negotiate with a jerk, keep the following in mind.

- **Giving up a little more than you normally would to a jerk is not selling out.** If giving up a little more means putting an end to this round of aggravation, do it.
- **Don't withhold visitation from a jerk.** Unless there is physical danger to a child, don't object to the jerk being around the children. First, while you might think the co-parent is a jerk, the children might not. Second, it is not written in any law that a co-parent you think is a jerk is not entitled to share time with the children. By withholding visitation you may be giving the jerk something reasonable and toothy to complain about. You can get in big trouble for that. Third, it is often true that for children, having a relationship with a parent who is a jerk is better than having no relationship at all.
- **Keep detailed notes and records of every aspect of you vs. jerk negotiations.** Should negotiations break down, you will find

yourself in front of a judge. While settlement negotiations are not supposed to be considered at a trial, judges often discover what offers went to the negotiation table and who rejected them before things fell apart.

- **Grit your teeth and kill with kindness.** If you smile and remain polite and respectful, the jerky characteristics will come to the forefront and turn off even the jerk's own representatives. Make the jerk's lawyer wish you were his client.
- **Stop calling the jerk a jerk.** Your perceptions and expectations will enhance all of the behavior that displeases you most. If you continue to call the jerk a jerk, you will not notice positive change or a softening of positions in your co-parent, and you have made her your enemy. Sometimes people cope with failed relationships by turning the co-parent they once loved into something repulsive and objectionable. It would be easier and more effective to turn your energy and attention to yourself, to stop punishing yourself for making a poor choice, and to avoid engaging in petty scorekeeping for the sole purpose of thwarting someone else's efforts.

The goal of negotiating any type of deal with any type of co-parent is to create a peaceful and equitable ending to the negotiation. You can do this by giving away small points, whether they be a few days of contact with your children here and there or some minor expenses on the financial front.

There can be something oddly comforting about focusing your attention on a co-parent who has become your enemy. It gives you an excuse to avoid other responsibilities in life. After all, almost everyone can be sympathetic to someone who is going through a rough divorce, especially where children are involved. But be forewarned: this coupon has an expiration date.

The unfortunate part about concentrating on your personal battle with the co-parent and putting everything else on hold is that doing so restricts you from bringing yourself into contact with positive change, new adventures, and a form of happiness and relaxation you probably haven't experienced in a very long time.

Finally, the more you refer to the other parent as a jerk, the more likely it is that your kids will hear you and repeat it. That will bring you even more unwanted trouble than you deserve, so don't do it.

Topic 9
How to Communicate with a Jerk

THE MAIN PRINCIPLES of communicating with an unreasonable co-parent are very much the same as the principles of negotiating with one. Here, however, I will focus on how important it is to detach yourself from all of the button-pushing that goes on during heated arguments. This includes preventing your attorney from engaging in similar types of nonproductive communication with another attorney. It is one thing to be aggravated by someone who is unreasonable and uncommunicative. It is adding insult to injury to pay someone to do it as poorly as you have done it. Here are some simple principles for communicating if your co-parent is a jerk.

> **Q**uick Tip: Respond to provocation by saying, "I don't want to fight. I'll be on my way in a minute." Then do what you came to do and move on.

Avoid Questions to Avoid Arguments

If there is a single piece of advice I could give to parents who argue with their co-parent, it is this: *Do not ask questions.* Questions invite sarcastic answers, and sarcastic comments escalate conflict. Here is an example:

> **Co-parent A:** How can you expect me to live if you won't pay me the money the court has ordered you to pay me?
> **Co-parent B:** Why don't you shake down your lazy boyfriend for some money? I'm tired of giving him a free ride.

Quick **Tip:** When you feel that your buttons are being pushed, understand that the sooner you get out of the situation, the sooner the hostile interaction ends.

Here is another example:

Co-parent A: Do you want our son to grow up without a father? Is that what you are trying to do?

Co-parent B: A father? Is that what you were trying to be? I'm sorry, I must have blinked and missed that part.

Make Your Requests Nonthreatening

Quick **Tip:** Monitor your body language and your facial gestures. Angry body language and nonverbal behavior increase tension. Smile, for your kid's sake—it won't break your face.

If you are trying to communicate something you need or something that must be done, do it with a short, nonthreatening request. Do not begin your request with the following phrases:

- I would like . . .
- I need . . .
- It is important that . . .
- I am upset . . .
- I am angry . . .
- You need to help me . . .
- You need to pay attention to . . .
- It is absolutely necessary that you . . .

All of these phrases invite responses that begin with phrases such as the following:

- What makes you think I care about what you would like . . .
- What makes you think I care about what you need—there are a lot of things I need that you don't care about . . .
- It may be important to you, but it isn't to me . . .
- If you are upset, then I am happy . . .
- If you are angry, that's too bad—try going to therapy . . .
- You need to help yourself . . .
- I need to pay attention to how to get you to stop bothering me . . .
- You may think that is necessary, but I don't . . .

If you give opportunities for sarcasm to your co-parent who does not want to engage in civilized discussion, the hostility will usually escalate and you'll fail to resolve the problem.

Quick **Tip:** Be the first one to end the argument. Give the co-parent the last word.

Another opening you should never give someone in an argument is *What do you expect me to do?* The almost universal answer to this question is *I expect you to act like a human being.*

Unfortunately, by this point in the conversation both parties are acting like human beings—and that is part of the problem. Many human beings do not know how to disagree in a civilized way.

Quick **Tip:** Stay outside of the co-parent's home unless you are told that you are welcome to enter. Intruding on the co-parent's residence, even if it used to be your home too, is an aggressive action.

Write a Note or E-mail Instead

When communication is poor, it is far better to communicate by writing a note in memo form, but only if you keep it short, businesslike, and neutral in tone. Here is an example:

> *TO: Michael*
> *FROM: Jane*
> *RE: Field trip to Washington, DC*
> *The sixth-grade field trip to Washington, DC, will be held on Thursday, May 28th. Ben should attend, and the cost is $65. I will lay out the total, as it is due tomorrow. Please forward your half of this fee to me in the envelope provided.*
> *If you are interested in attending as a class parent please contact Ms. Berger at 555-9876 by this Friday.*
> *Thank you in advance.*

There is no guarantee that the response to a note like this will be pleasant, nor is there any assurance that there will be a response at all, but it is possible. Be sure to always keep a copy of notes of this kind. Even if your co-parent's response isn't pleasant, notes like this will show that you were flexible and you provided the necessary information for the co-parent to participate as a class parent.

People arrive at the point of writing notes like this when face-to-face and phone conversations are nonproductive. Do not allow yourself to endure more than a few nasty conversations before you resort to this mode of communication. Hostile communications often escalate, and even when you can manage to get the last word in, they never make you feel good.

By writing e-mails, notes, and letters, you can choose your words more carefully and create a paper trail of your reasonable requests and your co-parent's unreasonable responses or lack of response. Often, people in conflict will not accept each other's mail. If that is the case, you may have to get your attorney to intervene.

E-mail communication can be just as damaging to the co-parenting relationship as verbal communication. Remember to mind your sarcasm and avoid the temptation to discuss multiple agendas in the same emails. Short and to the point is the rule here.

When All Else Fails, Let Your Attorney Handle the Communication

In the worst cases of hostile communication, it is best to have your attorney handle all communications. Taking yourself out of the loop is sometimes the only way to resolve issues that require communication and problem solving, while reducing your aggravation and negative experiences.

A word of caution: attorneys may not be altogether successful in communicating on your behalf if their style is to engage in aggressive letter writing campaigns to other attorneys. What often happens is that the attorneys who do not get along begin to fight and argue just as much as their clients. Consider the following pair of attorney correspondences:

> *Dear Mr. Belcher:*
> *Your client's relentless abuse and harassment of my client is outrageous and uncalled for. I would question the professionalism of any attorney who would support such egregious and acrimonious conduct as to deny responsibility for paying for a young boy's field trip to our nation's capital. My client, who is merely steps away from being kicked out onto the street, demands payment of $32.50 for Ben's class trip to Washington.*
> *Failure to remit within three business days will result in an immediate motion for contempt in front of Judge Jackson.*
> *Yours truly,*
> *Sidney Coffer, Esq.*

Dear Mr. Coffer:

It is your professionalism that is questionable if you think that a motion before The Honorable Judge Jay Jackson will solve this problem. I will seek sanctions against you as well as legal fees if you engage in thousands of dollars in motion practice for the sake of a $32.50 fee.

In the first instance, my client never agreed to split the cost of school field trips with your client. In the second instance, your client has more money than my client or I will ever see in this and the next lifetime. Your characterization of her being "merely steps away from being kicked out onto the street" is typical of the kind of histrionic exaggerations you and your client so frequently enjoy engaging in. The simple answer to your demand is "No."

Yours truly,

Edwin Belcher, Esq.

If these represent the type of correspondence that is going back and forth in an effort to facilitate problem solving and communication, perhaps it is time to start thinking about finding an attorney who can get the job done without being snookered into an ego war with her colleagues.

Topic 10
How to Keep Your Cool: Anger Management

There is a difference between someone who says, "Sometimes I get so mad I could spit" and someone who gets so mad he *does* spit. The first person can be helped by some sympathy and some good strategies for managing anger when being provoked. If this sounds like you, then the advice in this section will give you additional strategies to keep your cool so you don't lose control. The second person usually winds up with a restraining order, a few nights in jail, or, worse yet, killing someone—she has chronic anger or rage and needs help beyond what I can provide here. That is the difference between managing occasional anger and managing chronic anger or rage. Chronic anger is very difficult to change in a person, and most people who have chronic problems sincerely believe that it is the world at large who has the problem—not them.

> **Q**uick Tip: When you feel like screaming, lower your voice instead. It will get more attention. (Growling in a low voice or mumbling obscenities under your breath doesn't count.)

Anger is a very contagious emotion. When you come into contact with an angry person, it's often the case that you will become angry, or at the very least uncomfortable and uneasy. If you are in a high-conflict relationship with a co-parent, the anger generated by one person feeds the anger of the other person in a self-perpetuating cycle.

Quick Tip: Do not tell your personal business to people who will incite your anger and make you feel worse. Talk to people who will help you cope and move on with your life.

Understanding How Anger Is Destructive

It is always better to disengage or de-escalate hostile situations when you can. Anger and hostility generated by divorce and custody problems are destructive in many ways. The two most destructive ways are to shut down reason and to make you sick.

Anger Leads to Loss of Reason

Anger can lead to the point of complete loss of reason. That is a nice way of saying it can make you insane. Literally. The type of instability this sort of anger creates can lead to assault, even homicide. I have seen it more than a few times in my career—"normal" everyday people driven to extremes by anger at the ex-spouse or partner.

Intense anger like this breeds motivation for revenge. Revenge brings retaliation, and so it goes until one person raises the stakes high enough to either harm someone else or get caught and put in jail for trying to harm someone else. This is all separate from what it does to your children and your relationship with your children; it can and does ruin lives.

Anger Makes You Sick

Anger can make you sick, as well as ugly. Anger is a very corrosive emotion. It can erode your physical health. It certainly makes you age prematurely. It causes a type of ongoing agitation that advances your biological clock faster than the passage of time alone. No one really knows why, but there are theories stating that the type of agitation that anger and hatred causes places you in a state of frustration that builds and builds until it either bursts the vessel that holds it or gets released in the form of acting-out behavior.

This process causes the release of hormones that are associated with anger. Since the biological systems that control the release of these hormones were not designed to be "on" all of the time, if we tape those switches in the "on" position, we remain in a state ready to fight all the time at the expense of other biological processes that keep us healthy.

Strategies for Coping with Anger

Here are a few strategies that you can employ to help you cope with the kinds of anger that people struggle with in high-conflict divorce cases.

Handling Communication

If communicating face-to-face leads to an argument and to escalation of conflict, communicate in writing, by e-mail or voice mail, or with the help of an attorney. Sometimes face-to-face communication is unavoidable. If you must communicate face-to-face, bring along a friend—not the type of friend who is going to pump you up and encourage or even assist you in doing something stupid, but the real kind of friend who is going to stay in the background, reason with both of you and stop you from doing something stupid, or advise you to leave a rapidly escalating situation.

Use Your Support Network to Help You Focus on the Positives

When you build a network of supportive people around you and you are going through a rough time, all of your friends want to hear the latest "story" about your last fight or argument with your ex or soon-to-be ex.

Retelling stories of how you argued, were mistreated, of how you told someone what was good for them does not reduce anger—it increases it. That is because your friends tend to reinforce your side of the story and the things you did within that story. Encourage your friends to talk to you about the parts of life that you would like to get back to, presumably those parts that are enjoyable and do not involve daily battles. Friends should distract you from your angry conflicts, not assist you in investing in them.

Don't Stew Over What Happened

Related to the last strategy, do not replay your last argument over and over in your head. Do not rehearse what you should have said unless what you are rehearsing is a way to bring the level of conflict down. Do not imagine the other person dead, or killing the other person. There are different points of view on this. Some say, "Get it out of your system in fantasy, so you won't carry it out in real life." I strongly disagree. The more you think about doing something harmful to someone, the more you weaken your inhibitions against doing it. If you insist on fantasizing about doing something violent to someone, imagine yourself being caught and prosecuted for the criminal aspects of the behavior, as well as the consequences associated with the behavior.

Don't Invest in the Conflict

Examine the aspects of your life that are being brought to a complete standstill by your angry conflicts. There are consequences to your continued development as a person, consequences to your career, consequences to your ability to parent. High-conflict situations between parents tend to place everything else in life at a low priority—including, by the way, children. Even though people do not realize it, investing in conflicts tends to remove them from the responsibilities of day-to-day life. Soon, your conflict *becomes* your day-to-day life, and that is when it hurts you most.

You have a lot to gain by becoming less angry at the situation you are in. Do not let anyone else's desire to hurt you ultimately succeed in your doing the most damage to yourself.

When Anger Gets the Best of You

Try as you might, however, there are times when anger and frustration get the best of you. When that happens you must do some damage control. The first order of business is to correct any damage that was done to your children. Parents should not have to apologize to their children for every little mistake they make, but they should apologize for the big mistakes they make. This is even true when children do not realize parents have made a mistake. For instance, you are talking on the phone with your friend and you refer to your ex-spouse as a "bitch" or "bastard." As you turn around you notice your seven-year-old staring at you quizzically. Many people would rush the child out of the room and finish the conversation. Some people would not blink an eye and reason "Well, my kid's eventually going to find out what a jerk her father is anyway."

Both of these are very bad strategies. In a situation like that, get off the phone and tell your child that she just heard you doing something that you should not have done and that you are sorry she heard it. It does not matter that the other parent would not do the same if the shoe were on the other foot.

Your primary job as a parent is to teach. Parents teach their children all day long, every day. If you choose to teach your child to hate his parent, you are choosing to teach that child to hate others as well. You may find that when you teach a child to hate, that hatred might be turned against you. That is because you will be teaching your child to hate the things that displease him, and you will not always please your child, either. As a matter of fact, parents often have to go out of their way to displease their children because preventing them from doing certain things is important to their health and safety.

Teaching your child to apologize when she has done something wrong is a very important lesson. This is especially so when this is your primary complaint against the co-parent. So if the co-parent never admits he is wrong, and you never admit when you are wrong, what are the chances that your children are going to grow up and accept responsibility for the things they did wrong?

As in most cases, poor co-parenting makes day-to-day parenting a much more difficult task than it has to be, and as we all know, it is plenty difficult in the first place. When you make a mistake, own up and apologize.

Topic 11
Revenge: A Dish Best Not Served at All

THE SUBTITLE OF this topic is taken from the Sicilian saying *Revenge is a dish best served cold*. Aside from all of the moral and philosophical admonitions I could give you about revenge, the most practical reason to let the urge to retaliate against your ex fade from your emotional landscape is that revenge is almost certain to come back to bite you. In the context of high-conflict family difficulties the bite can be quite nasty—reduced time or supervised visitation with your kids, restraining orders, and possibly jail.

> **Q**uick Tip: Don't follow the co-parent around after an argument, especially if your child is around. There's a good chance you're going to be accused of harassing or stalking.

In order to succeed at revenge you have to be really clever and really, really patient. You have to be clever enough not to get caught doing something while you are dealing with the court system, and while lawyers and possibly other clever strangers (as well as friends, family members, new spouses, and your children) are watching your ex's back. Then, you have to quiet all of your other emotions—the disappointment, the anger, the urgency to even up the score swiftly—all of which rob you of the most important element of revenge, which is opportunity. In short, too many people know you and your motives, and the frustration of the situation you are in puts you in a bigger mess than you are already in—so don't seek revenge.

Quick Tip: Don't call the co-parent repeatedly and hang up the phone. In many states this is considered a crime, and even if it isn't, this behavior is not very gratifying and will probably get you in trouble.

Instead of trying to line up all of those planets only to give the other person a shot at going after you again, it might be best to focus on another quote—this one by George Herbert, a fifteenth-century clergyman and poet: *Living well is the best revenge.* Moving on from a horrible divorce, breakup, or battle over the kids is sometimes all you have to do to irk someone who has gone out of his way to make life miserable for you.

So many people report to me that an ex has ruined their lives. That seems hard to believe. Maybe they have harassed you for a portion of it; maybe they got more than you did out of the divorce or breakup. To permit another person to reduce your life to *ruination*—well, that's something that you have to participate in. You have to help that happen. You have to make your world so small and monochromatic that one person has the power to destroy it all. If that is so, problems with your ex are the least of what you need to get straightened out.

I am not saying you should settle for something grossly unfair, and I am not saying that you should forfeit a meaningful relationship with your children. Quite the contrary. I think you should do everything you can to show your kids you want to be an important part of their lives, as long as you do it in a way that is not a weak front for really hurting someone who has hurt you, because then you don't have your kids' needs in mind.

Sometimes, it is wise to lay back and see what the simple passage of time does for your predicament. I wish I had a dollar for every parent who was "alienated" from her child by a wicked and malicious parent, only to leave it alone for a while and have the kids come to her and tell her how horrible it was to live without her. There are no guarantees that this will happen in every case, but I have seen it happen often, especially when the alienated parent could point to a history of a loving and caring relationship with the kids before she was rejected.

And remember, laying off is not the same as "giving in" or "giving up." The difference is the difference between forcing opportunity and waiting for opportunity. You can only pull something unwilling to come to you so hard. When that doesn't work, let go and watch. You can always come back and fight; the courts are always there. If you permit yourself to lay back a little, you will often be surprised at how much movement things make on their own.

Part 2
Navigating the Court System

Topic 12
Do I Really Need to Be in Court?

HAVING TO GO to court, where a group of "important strangers" take hold of your time, your life, your children, and your finances, can be a very unsettling experience. Unfortunately, there are times when court is the only place that will give you the ability to move forward from a tense and possibly escalating conflict with your soon-to-be ex. People often ask whether there is a way to avoid court altogether. The answer to this is: rarely. In some cases your attorney can appear for you and represent what you want without your being physically present. You must almost always appear in court when there is a trial or hearing where you are going to be asked questions before a judge, hearing officer, or referee.

When You Need to Be in Court

You need to be in court if you are served with legal papers telling you that you must appear. Ignoring legal summonses and documents that require you to be in court usually creates difficulty on top of difficulty.

Quick Tip: Don't be an ostrich. Nervousness and fear can make you want to avoid looking at legal documents or responding to official papers. Deal with court papers sooner rather than later.

If you are embroiled in daily arguments with your spouse or co-parent, or if there is violence in the interactions between you and your co-parent, you would be better off in court.

Other factors that suggest you would be better off in court include the following.

• **You have an ineffective support system, or none at all—no friends or family members to serve as a sounding board.** In many jurisdictions you can find help for your legal troubles and concerns right at the courthouse. When you enter court, look for an information area; if you find one, state your problem in simple terms to the court clerk. It is always a good idea to have some notes with you, because people tend to get nervous in court even when asking simple questions.

Quick Tip: If you are absolutely unsure of what to do and have no access to legal help, go to the courthouse and ask whether there is a chief clerk's office. There are often people who can help you in the initial stages of a lawsuit right at the courthouse. This is almost always so of family courts.

• **You feel easily bullied by your spouse or co-parent.** Never try to negotiate for yourself if you feel easily bullied or pushed around by the person who is on the other side of the conflict. Court might be a scary place, but it exists to ensure that everyone is treated fairly.
• **Your co-parent is threatening to take you to court and drag you through the mud.** Contrary to what most people fear about being taken to court, most judges have a very low tolerance for personal mudslinging. Realize, though, that if you have committed a crime or have neglected your child and there is proof of it, that probably will come out in court.

When You Don't Need to Be in Court

It's possible to avoid court, or at least the worst parts of it, if you have a reasonable and civilized relationship with the co-parent and if your relationship is ending on good or friendly terms.

In that case you might want to try consulting a mediator or a mental health professional who can begin the process. The rules and protocols for how mediation takes place differ from state to state, so it is beyond the scope of this book to direct you anywhere specifically. A good place to start is by doing an Internet search for "divorce mediation" and to include the state in your search query.

Quick Tip: If communication is civilized, you might want to suggest mediation to your co-parent as a form of resolving your difficulties.

Still, even when you can agree on things there are times you must appear in court if only to swear or affirm in front of whomever is presiding over your case that you have indeed worked things out.

Topic 13
Preparing to Interact with Court-Appointed Professionals

IF YOU BRING your co-parenting problems into court, chances are you will be dealing with a lot of what I call "important strangers." These are people who are given the very awesome responsibility of managing decisions for you and your children that you cannot manage for yourself (if you could, you would not be in court). Some of these people include the following:

- Psychologists, social workers, and other mental health professionals (such as forensic psychologists)
- Legal advocates, law guardians, child advocates, and others who speak up for the needs of your children
- Probation workers and intake clerks
- Court officers, court clerks, and other courtroom personnel

Preparing for the Attitude of Court-Appointed Officials

All of these people do different tasks around the courthouse, but they can sometimes develop similar attitudes after working within the system for a lengthy period of time. You will probably detect this personality almost immediately. It is as if everyone you speak with is telling you the following: "What do you want? And when you tell me, don't try to put one over on me. I've already heard it all. Ask your questions and move on. Don't you know how bad an idea it is to bring all of your personal problems to this place?"

Quick Tip: Don't be shocked if your local court isn't the friendliest place on earth. Court employees can be stressed and frustrated by what "washes off" people around them.

This is a very insulting way to be treated, especially considering that you have never done this before and these people are supposed to be helpful. No one likes the way this attitude makes them feel, yet there are many people who work within the courts who rely on this attitude to cope with the stresses and strains of working in a demanding, unappreciative, and hostile environment.

Accepting the fact that you will be the recipient of some pretty cold attitudes when you step into most courthouses is not easy. However, not accepting this will often create more difficulty for you than is necessary. Let me explain.

People who work for the courts see the worst aspects of human behavior demonstrated all day long. I have worked in criminal courts, and I have worked in courts that handle family and marital problems and custody disputes (civil court). The only court I have seen stormed by court officers with weapons drawn was family court. The only court where I have seen a person spit in another person's face was family court. The only court where I have seen a man assault a woman, or a woman assault a man, was family court. In the course of my practice as a forensic psychologist I have interviewed criminals and noncriminals. I have had three attempted murders in litigants referred to my office. The perpetrators were custody litigants. There were two stabbings, both related to family conflicts. There was an assault four blocks away from my office in which a man was attacked because his ex-wife did not want him seeing his children. In all of the cases described, the perpetrators were all "regular people" indistinguishable from the woman squeezing produce in the grocery store, the businessman who sits on the train next to you, or any other friendly face you see every day. Even over time and with experience, people who do court-related work never develop the skills to determine who the good guys and the bad guys are. If you saw some of the people I have seen who have committed violent crimes in the middle of their family conflicts, you would know why—they are unassuming, businesslike, kind looking, mild mannered, and gentle in appearance. As a result of these experiences, there is a type of suspiciousness that develops in court-appointed and court-related professionals. Everyone is treated as a potential "bad guy."

This probably doesn't seem fair to you. If people don't know you, why should they treat you in a way that is rude, curt, or otherwise seemingly unfriendly? The first thing you should remind yourself of is that these people are not your friends. If you get angry while you are expressing yourself to a court officer, you may find yourself in handcuffs in very short order. If you yell at or threaten a court officer, court-appointed psychologist, mental health professional, or law guardian, you may find yourself being charged with criminal harassment, or possibly winding up on the wrong side of the judge hearing your case.

How to Interact Effectively with Court-Appointed Officials

Be Kind

My best advice is to kill everyone with kindness. If you do, you will see almost immediate results. As cold and hard as some court professionals might appear to be, many will drop the attitude when they conclude that you are not going to act out, cause a disruption, or attack them physically or personally.

> **Q**uick Tip: A good way to deal with grumpy court employees is to go out of your way to be respectful and gentle (almost apologetic) in your demeanor. It might not feel right to have to do, but it is effective.

Don't Cause a Scene

Another way of starting off on the wrong foot is to cause a disturbance in the hallway or courtroom itself. Courtroom stories fly fast and furious in the courthouse, and your behavior, embellished and exaggerated, will follow you throughout the case. You might think this is unfair, and you might resent the fact that losing your temper in the courthouse just one time will have a long-lasting effect on your case. But it will, so learn to count to ten.

Who's Who in the Court System

The roles and tasks of some of the most common court-appointed professionals are as follows.

Psychologists, Social Workers, and Mental Health Professionals

Psychologists, social workers, and mental health professionals are assigned to evaluate parents and provide information judges use to make a determination of custody. They can also be called a *forensic expert* or *forensic evaluator*. Sometimes the courts will assign mental health professionals as mediators who evaluate conflicts and suggest solutions, but do not provide evidence to the court at a trial or a hearing. Often, mental health evaluators are very important witnesses at trials on custody, because the opinions they provide are presumed to be neutral and will most likely strongly influence the judge's decision.

You might not like the fact that the court assigns a complete stranger to evaluate what goes on in your family. I don't blame you for feeling like this, but a mental health evaluation is often not optional: it is directed by the judge or magistrate, and it is required. Failure to comply with a court-ordered evaluation can cost you custody of your kids or result in a motion for contempt, which can be punishable by a fine or imprisonment. If you do not understand why you are being sent to a mental health professional, ask your attorney to explain it to you—do not decide on your own not to participate.

Evaluating techniques. Mental health professionals use a lot of different techniques for evaluating who the better custodial parent is. Some evaluations can take months to complete. Mental health evaluators rely on interviews, observations of parents and children, psychological tests, review of school and medical records, home visits, and contacts with friends and teachers to determine who the more appropriate custodial parent is.

You might wonder what mental health professionals "look for" when they are doing an evaluation. I cannot speak for every mental health professional, but I would be happy to tell you what I look for. I look for reasonableness. I look for parents who understand and appreciate the value of both parents in a child's life. I look for people who are civilized and diplomatic, people who can talk about what might make them uncomfortable about the other parent, but not so quick to characterize the other parent as a lunatic, a maniac, or emotionally unstable. When people describe their co-parent as emotionally unstable I start to wonder about what caused them to have a baby with this alleged lunatic. I am unlikely to believe, in most circumstances, that the person they are fighting with is an evil genius who hid a dark side for the first years of their relationship.

I am particularly sensitive to what parents seem to be saying to their children before the children see me for an interview. I almost always ask the children whether their mother or father told them to tell me anything. Once I asked this question to a five-year-old boy who thought for a moment, and then ran out the door into the waiting room saying, "My mother *did* tell me something to tell you about my father, but I forgot it. I'll be right back."

You might be very nervous about seeing a psychologist or mental health worker for an evaluation. I cannot blame you. Here is a perfect stranger who will spend relatively few hours with everyone in your family and then make a recommendation to a judge about the most important people in your lives. Some people prepare to speak to an evaluator by writing notes. I do not mind that at all. I also do not mind if people take notes during the evaluation or even tape the session, as long as they ask first and agree to provide me with a copy of the tape so that I can be certain it has not been altered. I believe that attorneys should be given as much information about the evaluation as possible, although jurisdictions vary from state to state as to what an attorney may be made privy to and what will only be seen by the judge or viewed in the judge's chambers.

What to do if you're not satisfied with the evaluation. At the end of an evaluation, you may feel as though you have not been evaluated accurately. There are a number of ways to deal with this. Ask the evaluator whether you may write a letter explaining your position on facts you believe the evaluator misunderstood or gave too much or too little weight to.

Communicate to your attorney aspects of the evaluation that you believe improperly cast you in a negative light. It is your attorney's job to show the court that an evaluator made a good decision or a bad decision about custody.

Quick **Tip:** If you are not happy with the evaluation you received by a court mental health evaluator, you can hire an independent expert to challenge the conclusions.

An evaluator's opinion is just that: an opinion. It does not have to agree with your opinion, and since the opinion generally favors only one parent in a contested custody battle, the opinion is at odds with at least one person's—yours or your co-parent's—point of view.

Law Guardians

The law guardian is usually a lawyer, but some states also use child advocates who are not lawyers. These people are appointed or assigned to make sure that the children's needs and feelings come to the attention of the court. When a law guardian is an attorney, that attorney can file lawsuits on behalf of the children, file motions, and call and examine witnesses. Law guardians usually provide the judge with an opinion on custody after the conclusion of a trial or hearing. Often a law guardian will participate in conferences or in chambers interviews of the children. The law guardian and mental health professional sometimes communicate with one another. Both are keenly interested in the well-being of a child. When the law guardian and mental health professional are in agreement with one another, this often has a very powerful influence on the judge's decision about custody, since the judge relies on the opinions of the professionals appointed to assist the court.

Probation Workers and Intake Clerks

In some jurisdictions probation workers may also be social workers and may provide the court with valuable background information as well as an opinion on custody. Probation department workers may take your fingerprints, do background checks for criminal records, or even search motor vehicle records. You must be very honest with these and other court-related professionals. Even a "white lie" about your past may be revealed by a computerized search and have an impact on how a judge views your credibility.

Court Officers, Court Clerks, and Other Courtroom Personnel

As I mentioned before, you may start off on the rough side of the people who manage the ebb and flow of people in and out of a courtroom. Simply maintaining a friendly demeanor, even with someone who has a stern tone to their voice or a grumpy attitude, will go a long way. There are some courtroom personnel who get a charge out of pushing people around, but there are far more people who will reach out and be very courteous and friendly to a person they have seen in the courthouse for a few days. Maintaining a pleasant interaction with courtroom personnel can go a very long way toward reducing your stress in the courthouse in general.

As with many situations in life, you can go through the court system grumbling about how victimized you are, or you can put your best foot forward and take control of the situation by being pleasant and respectful and waiting for your turn to talk. There is a very easy way to see whether this advice is correct. Go to court and watch what happens to people who cannot keep their attitudes in check or their mouths shut. They are usually the ones walking around in handcuffs.

Topic 14
Appearing Before a Judge

"THAT'S MY JUDGE?" people have been known to say once they see the waifish young woman, or the little old lady, or the Boy Scout leader, or the scruffy old man who will preside over their cases. Judges (also known as *referees* or *magistrates*) come from all walks of life, and they get to be judges in different ways—some by election, some by political appointment. They are all alike in one way, however: they wield a tremendous amount of power and can make your life miserable. That's the bad news. The good news is that I have worked for hundreds of judges in my career, and with the exception of just one or two, every judge I have worked for was earnestly interested in what is best for children.

After working in the legal system for a while, judges develop a keen sense for who is genuine and who is not. Judges are not always right, but they are always poking around for what is right. The laws that govern custody decisions are not as cut-and-dried as the laws that govern other aspects of human behavior. Most judges would prefer that Mom and Dad make the decision that they as judges are being forced to make, and most judges will give parents that opportunity time and time again. While doing so, the judge will assess who is reasonable and who is not, often through conferencing with attorneys and watching how people interact in the courtroom. I once saw a judge switch custody of a three-year-old boy who repeatedly tried to go to his father for attention and was thwarted by slaps on the hand and bottom by a mother who was trying to make it seem as if the child was merely misbehaving.

> **Q**uick **Tip:** Be very careful. Many judges can "see you" without directly looking at you and are very aware of your mood and demeanor in court.

What Not to Do in Front of a Judge

It may seem as if judges are distracted when they are flipping around through papers at the bench, but most good judges that I know can tell you everything that is happening in their courtrooms. This brings me to my first piece of advice about how to act in front of a judge: if you absolutely must do something stupid, discourteous, or hostile, do not do it in front of your judge.

Here are some other tips:

- Do not start an argument in front of a judge.
- Do not wisecrack or joke in front of a judge. It might not offend the judge, but the point is that you *do not know* whether it will or won't. So don't.
- Some people laugh nervously or joke when they are nervous. Do not do either.
- Do not chew gum.
- Do not appear before a judge in jeans or a ripped T-shirt. Wear nice, professional clothes.
- Do not go in your prom attire.
- Do not wear heavy cologne or perfume.
- When a judge speaks to you, look at her, *think before you speak,* and answer in the shortest possible sentence to get your point across. If a judge asks you a yes or no question say "Yes," "No," or "I don't know," and then add "Your Honor."
- Do not interrupt someone else, jump in when someone else is speaking, or blurt out, "He's lying." The most patient judges in the world will politely tell you three, maybe four times not to interrupt. After that, you may be warming up the bench of a jail cell.
- If you are being represented by an attorney, let your attorney do all of the "lawyer stuff." Do not act like an attorney. If you are representing yourself (which is not a good idea) and the judge seems to be ignoring your side of the story, wait for a break in the conversation and say, "Excuse me, Your Honor:

When it is possible, may I address the court?" If a judge denies you the opportunity to speak, it is either a very good or very bad sign. It is probably a good sign if the judge has not yelled at you for anything and seems to be perturbed at the person on the other side. If the judge does not want to hear from you in this case, it usually means, "Quit while you are ahead." Some judges will tell you this directly. If a judge will not let you speak and you have been making a nuisance of yourself, and the judge has been telling you to be quiet, it is probably a good idea to remain quiet and wait until the judge asks whether you have anything more to say.

- If you have done something that obviously offends the judge, apologize if you have the opportunity. Apologizing is different from "sucking up." Apologize by saying, "If I offended the court, I did not mean to, and I am sorry." Do not go overboard in an obvious effort to endear yourself by turning one simple sentence into a speech. Judges do not like to listen to speeches, from lawyers or litigants. A speech, by the way, is different from an explanation. A speech is self-serving and repeats the same point over and over ad nauseam. An explanation is when you answer a judge's question in a point-by-point manner. When judges ask you a question, they want you to answer the question they asked and not the question you *wish* they had asked. There is a difference, and judges know the difference. When a judge asks you, for instance, what you were doing in your living room when there was a stay-away order that instructed you not to be in the house, do not start by saying, "Well, Your Honor, my wife would not give me my baseball trophies and my hunting rifles, even after I asked her. She wants to ruin me and make me penniless and homeless. . . ." Similarly, if the judge asks you, "Ma'am, why hasn't your husband received his court-ordered visitation for the last three weekends?" don't answer, "Well, Your Honor, Mr. Smith has owed me $600 in unreimbursed medical expenses for more than four months." The correct answers to these questions are "I should not have been in the living room, Your Honor," and "There should have been visitation on those weekends." Most lawyers will tell you that judges already know the answers to a lot of the questions they ask—they just want to see if *you* know the answers to those questions.

Any lawyer who advises you to answer a question that has an obvious answer with an excuse is taking the chance of putting you in a bad position with a judge. There is a right time to bring up your agenda. Lawyers who understand this timing are usually great lawyers. Lawyers who don't get you in trouble.

Quick Tip: Be honest and not evasive. Lots of times, judges already know the answers to the questions they ask.

Giving Testimony Before the Judge

There may come a point when you have to give sworn testimony. If that time comes, you will be asked questions by all of the lawyers involved in a case, and probably by the judge. Good lawyers prepare their clients well in advance by helping them understand the types of questions that will likely be asked. Your lawyer will probably be asking the easy-to-answer questions. Other lawyers involved might try to make you angry or frustrated, or to twist your words. Do not try to outthink the lawyer who is asking you questions you do not want to answer. Do not try to outwit a lawyer or beat her at her own game. Lawyers can be jerks, but even bad lawyers have been asking witnesses questions longer than you have been answering them. Your best bet is to answer directly and truthfully. You are allowed to answer "I don't know," or "I don't remember," but if it is obvious that you are saying these things simply to avoid giving a truthful answer, no one will buy it, and by "no one" I mean primarily the judge.

It is better to look bad and honest than to be identified as a liar. Your lawyer will likely tell you what to admit and what to try to avoid admitting. I don't think it is a good idea to lie about anything. Nor do I think it is a good thing to "avoid telling the truth." Lawyers do not always advise their clients to be completely forthcoming. In the end, it is your choice. You can do what your lawyer tells you to do, or you can tell your lawyer that it makes you feel very uncomfortable to avoid answering certain questions or to lie. The bottom line is that lying from the witness stand is very risky business. In my experience, most judges are way too smart to be fooled more than once or twice.

> **Q**uick Tip: It is better to admit making mistakes than to lie about them. Most of us who work in the court system know that people are imperfect. As a matter of fact, most of us expect you to be imperfect and are suspicious when you seem too good to be true.

Your lawyer's mistakes and misbehaviors in the courtroom in front of a judge will ultimately influence the decision the judge makes about *you*. This is not true 100 percent of the time, but it is true enough of the time. Sometimes judges feel sorry for you because you are represented by an attorney who is making you look bad. Only you can determine whether your attorney's style is hurting your case, so pay attention. Your attorney may think your judge is prejudiced, biased, incompetent, or not paying close attention. It is up to her to overcome that with good lawyering and by adapting to the situation. As a litigant you should remain respectful to the judge at all times.

Always Be Respectful

I will close this topic with a story about a man who stood before a judge whom he did not think was treating him fairly. The man did not say a word, but was obviously examining and scanning the area of the floor under the table with his eyes. The behavior was so distracting that the judge asked the litigant, "Sir, what in heaven's name are you looking for down there?" The litigant replied, "I am looking for justice." Almost everyone in the courtroom chuckled, even the court officers. The one person who was not chuckling was the judge. Needless to say, that person did not fare well at the end of the case.

You cannot hurt the outcome of your case by being respectful to a judge. On the other hand, you can definitely hurt the outcome of your case by being disrespectful.

Topic 15
The Pitfalls of Taking Matters into Your Own Hands

SOMETIMES PEOPLE DO what they think is right or fair for themselves despite the court's warnings, admonitions, or orders against it. For instance, you might withhold visitation, thinking that your child is subject to poor parenting at the co-parent's house. This is often referred to as "taking self-help." Self-help is where you take it upon yourself to do such things as the following:

- Disobey a judge's order or directive because you do not think it was a good idea
- Schedule an activity for your child that runs over the co-parent's visitation time
- Move without telling the co-parent where you are going, terminating the co-parent's contact with the children
- Terminate visitation because you think your child may be in harm's way

Quick Tip: You might think you have the most reasonable excuse in the world to defy a court order, but when you do, you run the risk of being held in contempt. Get legal advice before you do anything that violates the court's orders.

You might have many good reasons for doing any of the things listed (and many other things that are not listed but fall into the same category), but you will work yourself into a lot of trouble in the process if your reasons are not extraordinarily sound. It is always best to consult your attorney before disobeying a court order or doing anything that severely interferes with your co-parent's rights. If you are worried about your child's health or safety, call your local child protective services hotline and discuss the situation with them.

Enlist the Help of Professionals

Your first way of checking whether your reasons for doing something that contradicts a court order or reduces or eliminates contact with a parent who has visitation rights is to discuss your plan with an attorney who knows something about family law. Discussing your plans with an attorney who is not a family lawyer is risky. If you get bad advice and act on it, you most likely will still be to blame in a judge's eyes. Just ask the mother of a young child who was told by an attorney who did not specialize in family law that she could move from New York to California, only to be served with a writ of habeas corpus demanding she return to New York. She lost custody of the child immediately on her return. The fact that her lawyer, a friend of the family and not a family lawyer, told her she could do it did not matter to the judge. If you think your child is being abused or neglected and stop visitation because you fear the child is in danger, seek consultation with a professional who knows something about child abuse, and call the child abuse hotline to ask whether the behavior and signs you are seeing suggest that your child is being abused or neglected.

If you terminate visitation with the visiting parent because your child says "it's boring," or doesn't like the food, it is likely that your behavior will not be viewed as being in the best interests of the child. Likewise, if you terminate visits because the co-parent owes you money, you are on shaky ground to say the least.

Do not take any form of "self-help" without contacting someone who is very familiar with the legal system, or with the signs and symptoms of abuse, if that is the issue. You might very well be creating more problems for yourself. At the very least you will be distracting the court from the issue that has raised your concern by giving the other parent an opportunity to make an equally strong complaint about you.

When You Suspect Abuse

When you consult professionals about abuse, be very cautious. Get something from them in writing stating the reasons why they think the child has suffered some sort of abuse or neglect. There are good professionals and bad professionals. How do you tell the difference? A good professional will not always be so quick to accept your side of the story, and may want to contact the other parent as well. Obviously, there are times when the child may have marks or bruises that are consistent with abuse, and time may be of the essence. There are also situations in which contacting an alleged abuser may result in reprisals against the reporting parent and/or child. Any professional who sees your child and concludes that there is a possibility that the child has been abused is mandated to report the suspected abuse to the appropriate state agency. Be wary of any professional who examines your child, concludes the child might have been abused, and then tells *you* to call the state agency.

Your local hospital may have a special unit that examines potential child abuse. Your pediatrician should be familiar with the signs of both physical and emotional abuse or neglect. A mental health professional is not always the right person to contact if your very young child (under four years or not verbal) is showing bumps or bruises that you think might be from abuse. If your child is not old enough to provide a detailed verbal account of what has gone on, a medical doctor who knows the physical marks consistent with abuse is the better person to contact first.

Topic 16
How to Choose a Lawyer

CHOOSING A LAWYER is not easy and not foolproof. There are a lot of caveats that apply to this process. Even when a friend has had great success with a lawyer, you might not; the facts of cases vary tremendously, and a lawyer who had certain advantages in a friend's case might not have those advantages in your case. Good lawyers will tell you that right up front.

"Doing well" with a lawyer varies from client to client. In some cases, doing well means getting 100 percent more money in a financial settlement than you would have gotten with a less-skilled attorney. In other cases, doing well might mean that you spend only three days in jail instead of thirty days.

> **Q**uick Tip: Your lawyer might have been recommended with rave reviews from someone else, but remember that your case is only as good as the facts behind it. Not even the best lawyer can always make a silk purse from a sow's ear.

When you ask a lawyer what are the possibilities in your case, he should tell you the best-case scenario, the worst-case scenario, and the probable scenario. Any lawyer who talks about "wiping the floor" with your adversary is not focusing on all of the possible outcomes. No legal case can be predicted with absolute certainty.

After working with matrimonial and family lawyers for twenty years, I can tell you that the personalities of lawyers can vary—completely dysfunctional, reasonable but not pushy enough, assertive and highly competent, overly aggressive. I have encountered a significant number of bad attorneys, but the good ones are amazingly good and worthwhile. By the way, the good ones are not even always the most expensive ones.

An overly aggressive attorney may concentrate on winning in the overall sense and not pay enough attention to what is practical for the money you are spending on legal advice. For instance, spending thirty thousand dollars to protect three thousand is stupid.

Lawyers should not feed into unreasonable demands and positions of their own clients without discussing all possibilities and outcomes with the client. When lawyers go to battle simply because clients want revenge or retribution, your money starts to go flying out the window. Revenge is usually very costly. Pocket the money you would spend on revenge and go to Hawaii.

Quick Tip: Think twice before you seek revenge, even that which is sought through legitimate litigation. It's pricey and can be very unsatisfying.

There is a reason why lawyers are called "counselors at law." It is because they are supposed to "counsel" you about all possible outcomes, including the most reasonable outcome.

Interviewing Potential Lawyers

Word-of-mouth referrals are always a good starting point for interviewing lawyers, but you should *take your time* if you can. Choosing a lawyer is not something you want to do many times during a legal case. Second, third, and fourth lawyers have to be brought up to speed on cases, and that is a difficult task for even the best attorneys, not to mention the fact that it costs money.

Most attorneys are eager to listen to your concerns and your questions. Take advantage of this before entering into an agreement. After you sign on, you will most likely find that your attorney is not as accessible as you would like her to be. That is because you are not her only client. Some attorneys are never around for their clients. If you feel as though your attorney is not giving you enough attention, you will have to straighten that out before it becomes a personal struggle and a psychological issue between you and the attorney. I have seen clients grow to hate their attorneys, but worse yet I have seen attorneys grow to hate their clients. You would think that clients would not stay with attorneys who hate them or whom they hate, but it happens all the time.

Q**uick Tip:** Ask your attorney right up front what you can expect by way of his availability to speak with you.

Questions to Ask

Here is a checklist of questions to ask and information to go over with any new attorney. It may seem as if there are many questions, but your initial consultation is certainly the place to ask them. When lawyers want your business they tend to pay close attention and have more patience. After your first few meetings, your lawyer will have many other things to attend to in your case and in other cases. If you find your lawyer getting annoyed or defensive about any of these questions, that is a bad sign. Any prospective new lawyer should show a high degree of patience and accommodation to clients who are seeking such an important service. This will be your first opportunity to see whether your attorney's ego is too big to handle your case. Ask your questions, and if you are the shy type, tell your lawyer you are asking the questions because you are following the advice of a book you read.

Q**uick Tip:** Ask your lawyer plenty of questions before you sign a retainer agreement.

Fees

- Is there a fee for today's consultation (the initial consultation)?
- Can you tell me what a typical retainer is for my type of case?
- After the retainer is used, how are any additional fees paid?
- Do you accept credit cards?
- Once a fee is established, are you willing to work with me on a monthly fee payment schedule, or do you need the entire retainer up front?
- Will you advise me of any fees that are recoverable at the end of my case?
- What are your fees for copying?
- Can I do my own copying of large documents?
- What are your fees for telephone calls?
- What are your fees for legal research?
- Do I get charged a fee if you have to adjourn a case for personal reasons?
- At what intervals do you provide me with summaries of my charges to date?
- Do you ever use associates to go to court for you, and if you do, what are the fee structures for this?

Skill, Experience, and Competence

- How long have you been working in the field of law?
- Is your practice a general practice, or is it a specialty practice in family law?
- How long have you been practicing in this jurisdiction?
- Do you know most of your colleagues in this field?
- How do you get along with them?
- Are there any judges that do not care for you?
- Do you know my co-parent's attorney? How do you get along with her?
- Have you appeared before all of the judges in this jurisdiction who handle my kind of case?

- Do you know many of the court-appointed professionals who work in this jurisdiction?
- How many trials have you done in this area of the law and in this jurisdiction?
- What kind of experience do you have cross-examining experts in this field?
- What bar associations are you a member of?
- Do you do any writing or speaking on topics related to my case?
- Have you ever been sanctioned by any state bar association or other governing body that supervises lawyers?
- Have your former clients filed grievances against you?
- How many cases are you handling right now? Are you confident that there is enough time in your schedule for you to concentrate on my case?
- Are you a solo practitioner, or do you have associates?
- How much of the work on my case will be done by you, and how much will be done by associates?
- Do you settle or try most of your cases?

Keeping in Touch
- How do your clients get in touch with you?
- Do you have someone who answers the phone during the day?
- Do you have an answering service that can get hold of you in case of an emergency?
- Do you accept e-mail correspondence from your clients?
- If I feel as though I absolutely must contact you about something, what is the longest amount of time I would probably have to wait for a return phone call?
- When would you be expecting me to be available for meetings you may need me for?
- Is it your policy to review all correspondence with me prior to sending it out?

Miscellaneous

- What bothersome habits of clients would you like me to avoid?
- What can I prepare for you to make your job easier?
- How does my file get transferred if I need to seek a different attorney?

What to Look for During Your Interview

Bad Signs

Watch out for any of the following bad signs:

- The attorney gets annoyed because you are asking too many questions.
- The attorney gets defensive when you ask if people have filed grievances against him. Most attorneys who have practiced for any appreciable period of time will have grievances filed against them, especially grievances over fees. The grievances aren't as important as disciplinary actions like license suspensions, but it is the attorney's attitude that you should be taking note of.
- The attorney picks up "important calls" every five minutes.
- Repetitive self-promotion. The attorney should not be trying to "sell you." I would not consider bragging a good sign.

Good Signs

Look for the following good signs:

- Straightforward answers
- A nondefensive attitude
- Taking time explaining answers, then asking at the end whether you have any more questions, even if you have already asked a lot of questions

- A feeling of comfort generated by the attorney's way of dealing with you
- Not making promises, but looking into all the facts of your case and keeping you apprised of your options along the way

What to Look for in an Attorney

Aggression is not the best trait you can find in an attorney, although people sometimes want a "bulldog" to fight for them. Attorneys who are aggressive are sometimes protecting king-sized egos. They often do not get along with the people they work with. They can be disliked by judges. Attorneys can be strong advocates without being scary and ferocious. They do this by knowing the law. Perhaps the media gives people the impression that good attorneys are dramatic individuals who have a Svengali-like ability to coax the most hardened liar to repent and tell the truth. Nothing could be farther from the truth. People lie in court and get away with it all the time. No judge can measure the truthfulness of what a person says when it is just one version of events versus the other.

Assertive and zealous representation is not always demonstrated by courtroom antics and hallway confrontations. It is demonstrated by good strategy, preparedness, and a thorough knowledge of your side of the story and the law that supports it. Everything else is just fluff and self-promotion on the attorney's part. Some of the most famous and popular "media lawyers" I have worked with have shamelessly misrepresented their clients by poor preparation, sloppy presentation, and skating by on their media hype. This will get some people far along in a case, but when this type of lawyer must deal with a less flashy but more competent, studious, and prepared lawyer, it is no contest.

Tips for Evaluating Attorneys

A good way to evaluate attorneys is to watch them work. It is often a good idea to seek a lawyer who specializes in family law and is a regular player in the jurisdiction where you are going to have your lawsuit.

Watch to see how much time the attorney spends with the client versus how much other business he is trying to handle at the same time. Keep in mind that there is a lot of downtime in many family law jurisdictions, and attorneys *must* conduct other business when they can. It is relatively easy to see, however, when an attorney is ignoring a client or, worse yet, scolding the client or talking badly about the client to another attorney. The last thing you want to worry about in the middle of a lawsuit is your attorney bad-mouthing you to other lawyers in the hallway.

Spend some time observing how other attorneys interact with your prospective lawyer. Do they seem to respect him? Do they immediately engage in arguments with him? Does the attorney appear to have good social skills? This can be very important during a phase in your case where it will become more important to negotiate than argue.

Topic 17
How to Get Along with a Lawyer

ENTERING INTO A contract with a lawyer in a family court matter is different from hiring someone to put aluminum siding on your house. Your lawyer sees you in a vulnerable state. Your lawyer is someone you rely on to make you feel protected, less stressed, and more confident that the legal problems you are having now will one day be over. Your relationship with your lawyer is a personal, emotional relationship, even though it is professional.

Your relationship with your lawyer can be healthy or unhealthy, depending on how the relationship is structured from the beginning. You will have needs in your relationship to your lawyer.

Your Needs

Your primary needs are most likely as follows:

- To be made aware of important information
- To be informed of any risks to you
- To be assured that your lawyer has adequately prepared to argue on your behalf
- To be assured that deadlines for submission of documents are met and that you are not unfairly penalized for delays or penalties caused by your lawyer's poor organization or performance
- To be assured that your lawyer will show up for court dates in a timely fashion (This is the number-one pet peeve of most judges I have worked for. If your lawyer is late for court, assume the judge will get irritated—and that can affect your result.)

If your lawyer is meeting these criteria, she is probably doing a good job in other areas as well.

Quick **Tip:** While your lawyer should be available to you in case of an emergency, don't expect any lawyer to hold your hand or coddle you. That's just not a reasonable expectation.

Your Lawyer's Needs

Your lawyer has needs, too. These needs include the following:

- Freedom from multiple phone calls about the same topic, or other forms of attention-seeking behavior that do not assist him in the performance of important tasks
- To be exempt from blame for events that are beyond her control—for instance, when you take a day off from work to go to court, only to be told your case is adjourned for something having nothing to do with your lawyer
- To be paid on the schedule you arrange with him at the beginning of the case. Your personal life and your future are important to your lawyer; however, when lawyers do not get paid on the schedule you promise to pay them, that starts to affect their personal lives, and that limits their ability to help you. It causes them to resent you, as well.

Most good lawyers do not like to be dictated to or told how to do their jobs. This does not mean that you do not have the right to ask questions about how they do their job or offer your suggestions. Striking this balance has more to do with *how* you communicate as opposed to *what* you communicate. For example, instead of telling a lawyer what she *should have* done, try asking whether there is a reason why a particular approach should or should not be taken. Your attorney should be more than patient with any civilized discussion you engage him in, if ultimately it makes you feel more comfortable.

Although very few will admit it, most attorneys love to be told they did a good job. Most people like to be told they are doing a good job. Lawyers are almost never told when they are doing a good job, even when their work is outstanding. That is because at the end of even a good day in court, they have always experienced some measure of aggravation. A little praise to your attorney will go a long way. This even applies to lawyers who cannot seem to stop talking about how wonderful they are.

Lawyers, like most professionals, can have a difficult time turning off their "lawyer personality." Part of this personality may reflect stubbornness, arrogance, or other objectionable personality characteristics. Remember, some of these same characteristics form the basis for their success. As long as your lawyer respects you, do not feel as though you have to love her personality.

Topic 18

How to Tell Whether Your Lawyer Is Doing a Good Job for You

A GOOD WAY to start gauging your lawyer's performance is to be sure you know exactly what you are going to court for on any given day. Ask beforehand what would be a good outcome, a bad outcome, and a likely outcome. If your lawyer tells you he has no idea, ask whether he is saying that so that you are not disappointed, or so that he does not get your hopes up. Some people would rather know the bottom line, even if it is probably bad. If that is your style, communicate that to your lawyer.

Sometimes your lawyer will tell you that she is having a difficult time "reading the judge." This is not a bad thing. Oftentimes in family law, judges make temporary rulings that seem to come out of nowhere or do not make sense. Some judges are known to be somewhat conservative in their rulings, and some are downright capricious. Your lawyer cannot be blamed for not being able to read the judge's mind.

Listen carefully to what a judge says to your lawyer in the courtroom. If a judge tells your lawyer that he was careless or failed to make the right motion or argument, ask your lawyer (after court) what the judge meant by those comments. If you start hearing things like that every time you go to court, it is a safe bet that your lawyer is either not getting along with that particular judge or is not adequately representing your needs. You might want to hire a different attorney.

> **Quick Tip:** Your lawyer should almost always be able to give you a best, probable, and worst scenario for what is currently happening in your case.

If you go to court and get more than half of what you have asked for, you are doing pretty well. People rarely get everything they want in court. Judges are very motivated to be fair. Popular psychology and common notions of fairness usually dictate that what is fair is what is divided equally or equivalently. Although the law might not say that 50-50 is fair, after observing judicial decision making for more than a decade, I can say that this is the rule of thumb that applies most of the time. When the 50-50 rule does not apply, most judges will make certain that everyone gets a little and gives a little in the spirit of compromise.

There are exceptions, of course, but popular wisdom dictates that a fair resolution to almost any problem is when each person gets a little of what they want and gives up a little of what they do not want to give up.

The generalizations I have made here do not apply when one or more aspects of your case represent an egregious violation of the law. Do not, for instance, expect to get a generous visitation schedule if you have run away with your child or were just arrested on drug charges. Judges try to divide time and parenting privileges equally when both parents are good parents who have shown that they love and care for their children.

Topic 19
When You Want to Fire Your Lawyer

YOU DO NOT have to have a fight with a lawyer before you fire her, although people often separate from their lawyers with the same intensity of emotion as when they separate from their spouses or partners. That is because your relationship with a lawyer can be very emotional and personal.

How to Fire Your Lawyer

As personal and intense as emotions can get, your relationship with your lawyer is a business relationship, and you can separate from your lawyer in a businesslike way simply by saying, "I do not think I can feel comfortable with your continuing to represent me. I would like to be represented by someone else."

Lawyers, especially seasoned lawyers, should not be offended by this comment. Sometimes a fresh look and a fresh face can make a big difference in a case. Opposing lawyers get on one another's nerves, and sometimes a new lawyer will get along better with his adversary. Please be aware that the lawyer you substitute might have a more hostile and contentious relationship with your co-parent's lawyer. There are no guarantees. An important question to ask any attorney you plan on substituting for your present attorney is whether she gets along with the other attorneys in the case. The reason why there might be more than one attorney-attorney relationship to consider is that the court may appoint an attorney to represent your child. This attorney is sometimes called a *law guardian* or *legal guardian*; in some jurisdictions this person is called a *child advocate* and might not be an attorney at all. Nevertheless, since you know who the other attorneys or people you will be dealing with are, it becomes important to ask any new attorney whether he has a good working relationship with these other professionals.

Separate on Good Terms

A very good reason to separate with your attorney on good terms is so that she will be cooperative with the next attorney. For example, problems can occur if your old attorney does not forward the case file to your new attorney. Attorneys will sometimes hold onto case files if your bill is not paid. This can make life very difficult for you and your new attorney.

Ask Ahead of Time

It is a good idea to ask any prospective attorney you are dealing with what procedure he follows for turning over case materials if you decide to be represented by someone else.

Topic 20
When You Want to Complain About Your Lawyer

SOMETIMES CONFLICTS WITH attorneys go beyond a falling-out or a loss of confidence. Attorneys must follow a code of professional ethics. When these ethics are violated, you have the right to file a formal complaint or a grievance against an attorney.

Although people have the right to complain about anything to anyone, grievances should be supported by information that suggests the attorney violated an important and well-established ethical principle. In most states, misappropriation of escrow money and failure to advocate for a client are grievable offenses.

> **Q**uick Tip: It is often best to speak with another lawyer before filing a grievance against your present lawyer.

A simple word of caution when considering whether you should file a grievance against an attorney: if an attorney has stolen money from you or otherwise taken advantage of you, or if an attorney's incompetence has had a profoundly negative effect on your life, you will be doing the world a favor by trying to limit this person's ability to practice. However, if you have merely gotten angry or disappointed with your attorney, you might want to think twice about filing a grievance. There should come a point at which you will want to be free of the legal system and all of the stress and strain that come along with it. Pursuing legal complaints and litigation should not become a full-time job. If that is the case, you would be better off going to law school and learning how to do it right (and getting paid for it).

For some people, getting wrapped up in legal struggles is a convenient way of avoiding responsibilities in "the real world." After all, if you are always in court, always complaining about your co-parent, always seeking some kind of relief for a wrong that was done to you, and complaining about your attorney, no one will criticize you for not managing the humdrum aspects of life that plague us all, whether we are embroiled in legal conflicts or not.

Remember, there is another life out there, beyond lawyers and beyond the people we no longer want to associate our personal lives with.

Part 3
Co-Parenting Successfully

Topic 21
Telling Children About Divorce

THERE ARE ONLY two kinds of messages that parents give to children regarding their divorce: positive and negative.

The Positive Message

The first message is a version of the following statement, which should be told to a child in as relaxed an environment as possible, at a time when being interrupted is unlikely.

> *Your [mother, father] and I are not going to be living in the same house anymore. It is better if we try to be friends from different places. We know that this will make you sad, because it makes us sad. We are both sorry that this has to make anyone sad, but sometimes things that are sad now turn out to be better when some time goes by. We are going to try our best to make sure that whatever we do, we always let you know that you are important to us and that we love you and will always love you, no matter where we live. If you want to tell us you are sad about this, that is OK. If you want to tell us you are mad, that is OK too. We want you to tell us how you feel, and we promise we will try to make it so that you will spend plenty of time with both of us and that we will try to make you feel better, because we love you.*

Obviously, this message should be customized according to the circumstances and the age and level of understanding of the child. For most purposes, when children are between the ages of about five and twelve, these words will do just fine.

Delivering this message with both parents present is essential. Accepting a child's emotional response is also important. Realize that some children will appear to have no emotional response at all. That is because they are in shock or denial. The emotions will show themselves eventually, because they almost always do. Sometimes children show their emotions over being told of a divorce when it is very inconvenient for you to listen. You can take this as a sign that a child is angry as well as sad.

The Negative Message

The second type of message you can give your child is a bad one, but it is given frequently in high-conflict families. This message is a version of the following statement:

> *We are getting a divorce because your [mother, father] is a sick and horrible person. We can't live together anymore because [I hate her, she hates me]. You'll get to see your [mother, father], but it is a waste of time. [He, she] really doesn't care about you, and doesn't love you because [he, she] does not have the capacity to love. You would be better off if [he, she] dropped dead or disappeared.*

You may make the message a lot more subtle than this, or you may reinforce the sentiments in this message slowly over time. No matter how it's delivered, a negative message hurts your child.

How the News Will Affect Your Child

There is no complex insight that needs to be learned when deciding how to tell your child about a divorce or separation. Understand that the information will be upsetting, either immediately, or later, or both. In addition, you should realize that knowing her parents are getting a divorce changes a child's perception of herself, and that is always uncomfortable. Before learning about the divorce, the child goes to school as part of a "whole" family. After she learns about it, she goes to school feeling different about herself, about her place among her peers, and about the uncertain future that lies ahead.

From the point that you tell your child about your divorce, you are changing his life in a dramatic way. You and your co-parent should do everything within your power to make that adjustment easier on your child.

Topic 22
Changing Notions of Custody in Society

IT IS VERY important to understand a few things about the word *custody*. First, perceptions about how children should spend time with parents after divorce are different than they were, say, fifty years ago. Back then, when there were far fewer two-parent working families, and it was presumed that mothers would stay home and rear children, a mother had to be considered "unfit" to "lose" custody of the children. Today, the practical and economical realities of needing two parents working to make ends meet mean that when parents separate there cannot always be one parent at home taking care of the children.

Quick Tip: During visitation changes, try to make the very last thing you say to the co-parent something positive.

Second, fathers are seeing their roles differently than they were fifty years ago. Many fathers want to be equal or at least equivalent parents. They do not want to see their children merely on weekends. They want to be active participants in their children's lives and are willing to fight for the privilege.

Unfortunately, the more traditional roles of parents continue to prevail in bitter custody disputes. I find it fascinating that the comparative worth of mothers and fathers to children is a factor in so many custody cases in this modern day, but it is. Often, if an attorney thinks she can sell the position that a mother's love is more essential to a child than a father's love, the mother will have an advantage. In the worst of cases, babysitters are given priority over available fathers when it comes to being with the children. Obviously, if a parent is so defective as to be a danger to a child, contact with children should be limited, but this is far rarer a circumstance than what the motion papers of contested custody battles would have you believe. Civilized co-parenting encourages parents to take advantage of the fact that parents living in different houses can actually *help* one another when schedules change.

Because custody and child support often go together, attaching the term *custodial parent* to one parent can have everything to do with finances and not be related to relative custodial fitness at all.

The bottom line is that there are a myriad of factors that make understanding the term *custody* difficult and confusing for people, and on top of that, the legal aspects of custody can differ tremendously from jurisdiction to jurisdiction.

For the purposes of this book, *noncustodial parent* refers either to the noncustodial parent in the legal sense or the parent who has the children a minority of the time. *Shared parenting* refers to an arrangement in which responsibilities for child rearing are more shared than they are the domain of one or the other parent.

Custody Can Be Whatever You Say It Is

While some of these are terms of law, they are also terms of art. In practical terms, it doesn't matter what you call any arrangement as long as you agree on the meaning of the term and your children are happy. I cannot stress enough that when you develop a civilized relationship with a co-parent, you earn the ability to be flexible—and that is quite a perk. If you do not develop that civilized relationship, your life will become full of important strangers (lawyers, judges, mental health professionals) who will have to micromanage every aspect of your life—and that is always more stressful than laying down the swords and doing it yourself!

Live Up to What You Ask For

It is important for parents to understand the nature of limitations that employment and other responsibilities place on parenting time. If the children live with you much more of the time, your parenting responsibilities increase, and in some ways so do your co-parenting responsibilities. Your job as a parent becomes more difficult. You cannot and should not be an equal parent to satisfy your ego. You've asked for the time so you can satisfy your kids.

Topic 23
Co-Parenting Responsibilities of the Custodial Parent

AT VARIOUS POINTS in this book you will see the term *custodial parent*. This is a legal term. When it is used here it means the parent who has the children for the large majority of the time, whether it be for legal reasons or practical reasons. People can have *joint custody* or *shared custody* in which one parent manages the children's day-to-day lives for the vast majority of the time.

> **Q**uick Tip: Allow the co-parent to have access to information about school, sports, activities, and doctor's appointments. Even if you are the custodial parent, you are not the only parent.

Make Sure Your Children Stay in Touch with Your Co-Parent

The most important co-parenting responsibility you have is to make sure that your children stay in touch with the noncustodial parent. This does not necessarily mean daily telephone calls (see the topic on telephone contact), but it does mean to have the children keep in touch regularly, especially if the noncustodial parent lives out of town or far away.

Give Your Co-Parent Access to Important Information and Documents

Noncustodial parents, especially those who live out of town, do not always have access to school or medical records. I do not believe the custodial parent should act as a copy service and errand runner for the noncustodial parent. The custodial parent should, however, transmit names and telephone numbers of important school officials, doctors, and other professionals involved in the children's lives. Sending a copy of school report cards to the noncustodial parent is a nice gesture. Schools have different policies as to who they will send school records to, so if you know your school is stingy about sending more than one set of report cards out, make the copies and send them along.

One area of unnecessary conflict comes when school pictures arrive. School picture time might not be the type of information that normally gets transferred from parent to parent, but noncustodial parents usually become very upset when they are not offered pictures.

Important Responsibilities

There are some other important responsibilities of the custodial parent, including the following.

- Do not schedule events and activities over the noncustodial parent's time.
- Have the children ready to leave the house when it is time for visitation. Many noncustodial parents value every second of time they spend with the children. If you are the custodial parent, you are probably used to having the kids around and under foot. The parent who sees the children less is often more of a clock-watcher, and doesn't want to sit in the car for a half-hour waiting to see the children after waiting so long between visits.
- Do not send the kids to the co-parent dirty or in tattered clothes. The co-parent might have planned to take them some-

place immediately after picking them up and might not have time to get them cleaned up. I am not suggesting that parents usually send their kids to visitation dirty, but kids play in the backyard and get grungy. Make sure they are presentable when the noncustodial parent comes to pick them up.

- Do not start conversations about money or other "business matters" in front of the children during pick-up and drop-off, and do not send the children to the visiting parent with requests for money or other issues better left between the two of you.
- Whenever possible, offer to extend time with the children, especially when it seems that the children want more time. Honor reasonable requests when the co-parent wants to do something special with the children that falls outside of normal visitation time.
- Compliment the co-parent when the children come home happy and looking like they are having a good time. Tell the visiting parent that it is nice to see how much the children love him.

Quick Tip: Be flexible, and arrange makeup visits whenever possible.

Topic 24
Co-Parenting Responsibilities of the Visiting Parent

FOR THE PURPOSES of this book, *visiting parent* refers to the parent who sees the children for the minority of the time. Terms concerning custody can be confusing. A "visiting" parent might be a parent who has joint custody but sees the children less of the time. A visiting parent might also be a noncustodial parent who sees the child less of the time.

Quick Tip: If you have to cancel a visit at the last minute, first tell the co-parent, and then get on the phone with the child, explain, and apologize.

Certainly, many parents who see the children for the lesser portion of time want to see their children more, and do not because of either practical reasons (the children do not live close by, work schedule precludes it, and so on) or legal reasons (for instance, it is not part of the legal agreement or judicial order).

Keep Apprised of Important Information

The visiting parent may at times feel out of the loop with respect to things that are going on in her children's lives. The custodial parent should make an active effort to keep the visiting parent up-to-date with important information, but the visiting parent should make an active effort to get this information as well. For instance, you should not rely on the co-parent to send you every little piece of paper that comes home from school. Speak to the officials at your child's school and see whether they require any letters of consent or legal paperwork for you to be allowed to speak directly with your children's teachers. I think this is absolutely critical for noncustodial parents, because noncustodial parents often complain that they feel as though they are treated like second-class citizens. This need not be the case. As long as you do not make a nuisance of yourself, your children's teachers should be very happy to speak with you. If they are not, find out why. You may have to provide them with a letter of consent from the custodial parent, or a notarized document saying that you are permitted to have access to the children's teachers. The same goes for contact with your children's doctors.

Attend Extracurricular Activities

Sports events and other after-school activities often run on schedules that are generally provided at the beginning of the school year. Ask the co-parent to send you copies of the schedules that pertain to your children's after-school activities. Going to after-school activities and simply watching patiently in the background is a good way to see your children between visits. Be certain that you work this out with the custodial parent first, so that, at least from the co-parent's point of view, your attendance will not be a surprise.

Quick Tip: Clean your children's weekend clothes before you send them back to the co-parent.

Co-Parenting Tips to Keep in Mind

Here are some tips for keeping the co-parenting relationship on the right track.

- **Communicate briefly what happens during visitation.** This will help the co-parent understand the mood your children come home in after visitation. Sometimes visitation might make children sad or moody simply because it reminds them that their parents are not together. Other times it is because the children will miss the visiting parent, so they become sad toward the end of the visit.

- **Pick the children up on time, all of the time.** When you are running late, call in advance and say how late you will be. Sometimes the other parent will have plans that require you to be there on time.

- **Always call before you go to see the children.** Even if your relationship with the co-parent is exceptionally good, do not drop in unexpectedly to see the children.

- **Try not to bring the children back exhausted, riled up, or dirty.** Always keep a clean set of clothes for the kids with you, even if it is sweatpants and a T-shirt or sweatshirt. Bringing the children back exhausted or hyper means the custodial parent is going to have a hard time with them. It is always a good idea to have some quiet time before the end of a visit so that children can decompress before going back home.

- **Do not put your children in the very uncomfortable position of calling the custodial parent and asking to extend your time.** This makes the custodial parent look like "the bad guy" if he cannot extend the courtesy. If extending the visit does not inconvenience the co-parent, call and ask yourself. Sometimes, especially with young children, the co-parent might want the children to return home even when they have nothing in particular to do. Do not be so quick to assume that this means the co-parent is being rigid or stingy with time. Young children (under six) get accustomed to certain routines at certain times, and extending visitation might interfere with those routines.

- **Compliment the co-parent from time to time** on how the children are behaving, how healthy they look, or how well they seem to be doing.

Topic 25
Moving and Relocating

IT'S WIDELY THOUGHT that the three most stressful events that can happen in the life of a child are the death of a parent or close family member, divorce, and moving. If this is so, it would appear as though a move during or following a divorce would be adding insult to injury. Financial circumstances often determine the necessity of a move. Ability to survive and overall quality of life are certainly factors parents need to take into consideration.

There are, however, negative consequences for a child who is uprooted from family and friends needlessly because the custodial parent wants one of the following changes:

- To move closer to her new partner
- "A fresh start" far away from the noncustodial parent, despite the fact that the children enjoy spending time with that parent
- To separate the children from a parent out of malice or spite

Please remember that whenever you move a child outside of his school district you are forcing the child to adjust to new friends, new teachers, and new environments. These are sometimes the only measures of stability left in a child's life after parents divorce.

You might hear some say that children are resilient and adjust easily. This is true of only some children. Many children do not adjust easily and are frightened, saddened, or otherwise put off by change.

How the Move Will Affect Your Child's Relationship with Your Co-Parent

You must carefully consider changes in the children's pattern of contact with a noncustodial parent the children see regularly. Some parents who are separated by distance will try to replace the time the children are losing by adding more holiday and summer visitation. The math might work out the same, but the impact can still be very negative, especially if the noncustodial parent participated in school and extracurricular activities, was a coach for a sports team, or even had a regular weekend date with the child.

Sometimes divorced parents forget that the decisions they make create the psychological videotape that becomes their children's childhood memories. Is it better to have a few concentrated periods of contact with the noncustodial parent, or better to have weekend ice cream sundaes and all of the "little experiences" that form the basis of emotional memories that are more intimate and, in the long run, probably healthier psychologically? Usually it is the latter.

Many parents who move leave with the feeling that the children do not have much to gain by seeing the noncustodial parent on a regular basis. I believe this would be a very difficult thing to know with confidence. You would have to know what happens during every moment of your children's contact with the other parent; and to know this you would have to know what "really" happens as opposed to what your children say happens when they are there.

When You Are the Noncustodial Parent

If you are the noncustodial parent, and your children are moving away over your objections, it's important to avoid making your children feel bad about a decision they probably have very little to do with. This includes making them feel guilty and telling them that you will cry when you think about how far away they are. Instead, tell them that you will love them no matter where they live, and that, although you will miss them, you will do your best to call them, communicate with them, and see them. If you believe it is in their best interests, fight hard to have them stay nearby, but do not involve them directly in your struggles.

Know Whether a Move Is Legal

In the United States, no parent has the right to leave the jurisdiction of the court their case is in unless the other parent consents to the move or if there is a court order permitting it. I have worked on many cases where a poorly informed parent has packed up and moved to another state, only to be served with legal papers telling them they must return to their home state. This includes cases where the parent who has moved has, for all intents and purposes, been the only "real" parent in the child's life. One law that addresses the issue of moving is a federal law called the Uniform Child Custody Jurisdiction Act (UCCJA).

Topic 26

Co-Parenting in Medical Emergencies

A MEDICAL EMERGENCY is the most important time to communicate with your co-parent. Aside from the fact that your child's life may depend on a transfusion or other medical need that only the co-parent is able to fill, your child will feel less frightened and more secure if both of you are there.

Work out emergency medical contact procedures beforehand. Trade cell phone or pager numbers that can be used in cases of emergency. Make sure you have the name of a relative, friend, or family member who can get in touch with the co-parent if you can't. Remember that co-parenting requires cooperation. You will not be doing a sick or injured child any favors by arguing at a hospital or doctor's office. Aside from the stress it will cause for your child, you will interfere with medical professionals' ability to do their job.

If things get too tense, separate yourselves. If a doctor comes over to you first, call the co-parent over to listen to what she has to say, or direct the doctor to talk to the co-parent next.

If your child goes to the emergency room for any reason, do not wait until the next day, or "your next free moment," to call the co-parent. I have seen this type of situation create long-standing problems in the co-parenting relationship. Remember, your child's needs always come first.

You might be thinking, "I would love to be able to work this way with my co-parent, but I can't because he is completely unreasonable." All I can say about this is that there are a million reasons people can come up with for not being able to do what is best for their children. After the millionth reason has been given, the fact remains that when one parent is able to bite their tongue and do what is best for their children, *that* is what helps them most.

Topic 27
Telephone Contact Issues

> **Quick Tip:** Don't spend phone time peppering your children with questions about what they are doing. Most young children do not like to speak on the phone, mostly because they do not like to be interrupted from what they are doing. Learn to make appropriate "small talk." This is how a typical phone conversation should go: Say what you did; then ask how the child's day has been, and listen; then say, "I love you, and I will see you soon."

One of the most overemphasized negotiating points in custody conflict resolution is the frequency of phone contact with the parent a child is not with on any given day. The custodial parent might want telephone contact when the child is with the noncustodial parent. The noncustodial parent might want telephone contact one, two, even three times per day when the child is with the custodial parent. ("I should be able to say 'Good morning' to my child!" "I should be able to say 'Sweet dreams' to my child!")

Often in these situations, parents fear that they are not being given "their rights" with respect to their children. Telephone contact usually isn't the real issue here; rather, the issue is the right to intrude on the other parent's time and to control the other parent's schedule by making sure they are in the "telephone contact place."

It is nice for parents to be able to speak to their children by phone, but telephone contact with parents whom kids already see on a regular basis is not a crucial determinant of their mental health. This is true at age six and age forty-six.

Quick Tip: Prepare your children when it is time for a telephone call from the other parent. Say, "Mom [Dad] is going to call to see how your day went. When the phone rings I want you to stop what you are doing and talk for a while."

My experience has shown me that many children do not particularly like talking on the phone. There is a period in early development where children are fascinated by the noises phones make, and they want to imitate the adults who are using the phone. But most children older than four years do not want to stop playing to come to the phone and may be very fickle or obstinate about doing so, in spite of a parent's best efforts. At eight years old, children are self-conscious about what they say on the phone because they do not want to be overheard. By twelve years old, if the person on the other end of the phone isn't someone from school they just finished talking to five minutes ago, they do not want to get on the phone.

Quick Tip: Do not snoop on children's telephone conversations with the co-parent. If something bad happens during the call you'll hear about it soon enough.

Sometimes kids do not mind talking on the phone. That is a great benefit to the parent who wants to say hello. When this is the case, keep your phone calls brief, tell your child you love him, ask how school is, and then say "I love you" again and say good-bye. This process takes about five minutes.

Don't Use the Telephone to Harass Your Co-Parent

Parents sometimes use telephone contact as an excuse to harass one another. This is expressed in the following ways:

- Demanding unreasonable amounts of telephone time
- Demanding that a parent be in a certain place at a certain time for telephone contact every night
- Using telephone time as an opportunity to interrogate the children
- Recording conversations so that the child unwittingly becomes an instrument to get a parent in trouble
- Hanging up the phone when a parent calls and letting the child think the calling parent doesn't care about her
- Hovering over the child while he is on the phone
- Making your child feel bad about wanting to speak to the other parent
- Making your child crazy with the thought that he should be calling you, so that he panics when he cannot make the call for some legitimate reason
- Demanding that a child carry a "special phone" that is just for the purpose of receiving calls from the other parent
- Telling your child, "That's enough, get off," and then removing the phone from the child's hand
- Demanding that a child "check in" when on visitation so that the custodial parent knows the child is "safe" (If you are genuinely worried about this, you should be appearing before a judge who can determine whether the visiting parent should have supervised visitation or whether you are overprotective and inciting fear in your child.)

When co-parenting relationships are bad, don't expect even simple things like telephone calls to be easy to set up. If you tell your child you love her often enough, she will not need to hear it on the phone. If you do not put pressure on your child to call because you know the co-parent makes an issue of it, you will be doing your child a favor he will appreciate.

Good phone contact is a few times a week between visits or shared parenting time. It doesn't have to be every day. If it can be every day and everyone is happy, that is fine. Do not expect your children to give you a minute-by-minute itinerary of everything they did during the day, and do not use your telephone contact time for "intelligence gathering" in your custody war.

Topic 28
The Importance of Sharing Information

ASIDE FROM SHARING medical information and school information, it's important to understand the need for parents to develop a habit of sharing information.

Three Types of Information

Information about children between co-parents comes in three basic forms or types: good news, bad news, and just news. When co-parenting relationships are poor, most of what is shared is bad news, and the bad news is some bad thing that happens to a child that somehow is the fault of the one receiving the news. There is no need to go into great depth about why this happens. In poor co-parenting relationships, everything is always the other person's fault—poor spelling grades happen because there is no follow-through from the co-parent; bad behavior or trouble in school happen because the co-parent has ruined the family.

In poor co-parenting relationships, good news is shared only when the bearer of the good news can eliminate any joy that the receiver of the good news may get from it, and the news is punctuated by the phrase or insinuation "No thanks to you."

In poor co-parenting relationships, just news (neutral news) is not presented at all, or is turned into bad news, along with the typical blame of the recipient. Often it is withheld completely because one parent does not think the other has any right to information about the children.

Share All News, All the Time

If you want a good co-parenting relationship, you must get into the habit of sharing all of the news all of the time. Positive information should be shared with the implicit message "We are both doing a good job of raising our children, and I want to thank you for your part."

Neutral news should be presented as a matter of courtesy and respect, and to affirm that information about the children is important for both parents to know. The other reason to share the neutral news is so that everything that is discussed about the children is not either really good or really bad. Since even the best co-parents do not interact on a daily basis, it is not a good idea to learn to expect that any information about the children will be either "good" or "bad." Neutral news permits parents who do not have as much contact with the children to feel as though they are keeping up with all aspects of their children's lives, not just the highlights or the lowlights. Finally, sharing the neutral news prevents the perception that the only time information is shared is when there is a problem and the co-parent wants you to do something about it.

In good co-parenting relationships, sharing bad news is often a way of soliciting help, and that is a good thing—two heads are better than one. When sharing bad news, be sure to thank the co-parent for listening and for offering to help; and when receiving bad news, thank the co-parent for sharing and for affirming the importance of your contribution to your children's lives.

Topic 29
Self-Defeating Behavior: Overprotectiveness and Rigidity

THERE ARE TIMES when a parent is so, so sure that his co-parent is toxic and horrible that he refuses to believe the co-parent can provide anything of value to a child:

- "She is just a playmate."
- "She is too irresponsible to raise a child."
- "She won't supervise my baby well enough."
- "Who is going to take responsibility if I let my baby visit and the baby gets hurt because she can't handle the situation?"
- "She couldn't properly care for a goldfish, let alone a child."

I have heard these sentiments more times than I can count from parents who have been repeatedly disappointed by the behavior of their former partners.

Quick Tip: When a child returns home from visitation, let him settle down. Do not ask any questions, no matter how innocent sounding. The last thing a child wants to deal with is questions as soon as he walks through the door.

Often what it boils down to is the custodial parent does not approve of the visiting parent's style, safety precautions, and family values; and, as a result, she overanalyzes what children (especially young children) say and do after visitation.

> **Q**uick Tip: Do not encourage your children to keep diaries and written records about how horrible their mother or father is. Parents often do this to assist their litigation. This causes the child to feel as though he is under pressure to chronicle every negative thing that happens. This intensifies anger and alienates the co-parent. Do your best to repair poor parent-child relationships, not make them worse.

When I suggest to overprotective parents that they are being overprotective, they often get very angry at me and say something like "Does something have to happen to my child before anybody does anything about it?"

> **Q**uick Tip: Do not try to teach your children all about the co-parent's faults and problems. Children eventually discover their parents' flaws on their own.

Not necessarily, and that's when an impartial court investigator or evaluator can be really helpful—but only if you are willing to listen to what that individual says. More times than not, when I evaluate a visiting parent to determine whether a custodial parent's concerns are valid, my evaluation is rejected by the custodial parent unless it conforms fully to her opinion.

A deficient parent can "put on a show" for the court and appear to be a better-equipped parent then he really is. However, in a court setting, the goal is fairness to both parties. One parent is not allowed to judge the other parent and subsequently determine visitation or the conditions of visitation. It might be true that you know the situation better than anyone else, but if you were permitted to make all of the decisions there would be no need for a judge.

Defaulting to the decision making of judges, law guardians, and mental health professionals is the natural consequence of not being able to work things out parent-to-parent. The court system and the people in it are going to try to be fair. It doesn't always work. Sometimes "the bad guy" gets too much attention, and sometimes the "overprotective parent" gets to have too much say in restricting the other parent's visitation unfairly. Still, I believe that most times, good outcomes are achieved.

It is hard to convince people that they might be too close to a situation to be assessing it accurately. Rigid and overprotective parents do not understand this and defend their overprotectiveness on the grounds that a judge or evaluator cannot possibly know what a maniac the co-parent is.

One liability of being overprotective and very vocal or assertive about it is that without solid evidence to justify your concerns, you run the risk of being seen as someone who is merely manipulative and controlling. When this happens, the decision makers around you might be very put off and conclude that as long as you are in control, the other parent is not going to have an adequate place in the child's life. You could then face a situation where the visiting parent might get a lot more visitation and contact than she would have before—or, worse yet, a loss of custody altogether. This does not happen often, but I have seen it happen enough times to warn people that rigid and overprotective parents should be concerned about the consequences of that behavior.

A good approach is to demand a parenting evaluation if there is not an evaluator appointed already, and if there is an evaluator, try to remain open to feedback and suggestions.

Part 4
Divorced Parenting for Ages and Stages

Topic 30
Special Needs of Infants

COMMUNICATION IS ALWAYS important between co-parents, but it is especially important when trying to raise an infant. Infants' needs change frequently. They are more likely than older children to have special medical, diet, and clothing requirements.

Communication

If you cannot communicate in a civilized face-to-face manner with your co-parent, communicate in writing about the changing needs of your infant. If you are the custodial parent, it is never a good idea to withhold the name of your child's pediatrician or any other medical professional from your co-parent. This happens frequently, and it is a disservice to the child. It is dangerous to leave a parent off an emergency contact list, especially if that parent has access to medical history information important to your child's health.

Doctors should feel comfortable talking to both parents, but do her a favor and leave her out of your legal troubles. Do not subpoena records or threaten to bring your doctor into court to testify to what a lousy job the co-parent is doing raising your child unless there is a clear record of child abuse and your doctor has seen and recorded the signs of it. If you drag the family doctor or pediatrician in for no good reason, you will most likely lose the services of this professional before long. Common sense dictates that when someone is providing medical care to your child, you should treat that person courteously, but common sense often is in short supply when people are engaged in an acrimonious co-parenting relationship.

Keeping Both Parents Involved

Do not assume that one parent is more important than the other. New fathers cannot be expected to develop bonds with their infants if they only see them for an hour each week. When new fathers are relegated to one hour per week of contact with their infants, they are often denied visitation when they ask for more time because "the baby has never taken to him and does not feel comfortable around him." This puts fathers in a very tricky position. First, the father is sequestered from the child, seeing him only once a week for an hour or so. Then he is blamed for not being able to establish the proper bond with the infant. Fathers play an important role in infants' emotional development that should not be ignored.

> **Q**uick Tip: Provide written instructions to the co-parent on how to dispense any medications that might be necessary.

Infants experience developmentally predictable separation anxiety. This usually occurs at six months, and again around eighteen to twenty-four months. I have seen mothers have no trouble leaving their crying infants in the capable care of a maternal grandmother, but absolutely refuse to allow a father anywhere near an infant on the criticism that "the baby cries when she goes to her father."

Fathers sometimes make a bad situation worse by expressing their frustration with statements like "You are keeping that baby away from me—I will make it so you never see him again." This is not the best way to approach a possibly overprotective mother with respect to your new infant. Communicate that you want to cooperate and that you understand she may be nervous with the new baby. If you are the father of a new baby, please understand the importance of a mother's bond with an infant and respect that this is a very emotional time and very difficult for her when it is time to separate from your baby for any reason.

Let's look at it this way: if you are separated or divorced and you have an infant, realize the baby may already be starting life at a place that requires more tenderness and understanding.

Handling Custody and Visitation

The best way to manage custody and visitation of an infant is to permit the visiting parent to come into the custodial home and interact with the infant a little every day. This way the child is in contact with both parents in a comfortable, familiar environment. Your child does not have to be subject to the stresses and strains of too many transitions. After the child is six months old, a day away from home or an occasional overnight visit can be successful if the child has the type of temperament to easily adjust to the change.

Eighteen months (preferably after the child's separation anxiety passes) is a good age to start scheduling regular overnight visits. This age will vary based on the natural or inborn disposition of your infant. Parents, please remember: your infant's mental health is not about you, your failed relationship, or the things your ex-partner did to make you irritated or angry when you were together.

Do what is best for your baby. The first few years are not easy. Babies need a lot of attention. Some babies react poorly to change, especially those who are fussy, colicky, or regularly sick. It isn't worth taking the infant out of the primary household just to prove something. You have the rest of the child's life to prove that you can manage him in your home. For now, see if you can structure the child's time mostly in one place until the eighteenth month or so.

Topic 31
Special Needs of Toddlers and Preschoolers

TODDLERS AND PRESCHOOLERS are at an age where they are first coming into their own. They are expressing their independence and often their fickleness. In an intact family, were a toddler to say, "I don't like Mommy," neither parent would give it a moment's worth of serious consideration. But when parents are divorced, such statements can be distressing to parents. A toddler might say she doesn't like Mommy or Daddy simply because everything in her world is subject to a thumbs-up or thumbs-down evaluation depending on whether she is being allowed to do what she wants at the time. By the same token a toddler might state that he does not like Mommy or Daddy because it is time to take a bath and he doesn't want to be interrupted from what he is doing.

Keeping this in mind will help prevent you from drawing erroneous conclusions about what happens when your toddler is in the other parent's care. If you hear something from your toddler that sounds unsettling, reach out to the co-parent by saying something like "Mary mentioned something to me after coming home from your house. It was a bit confusing, so I was hoping we could discuss it."

Concerned parents should be very willing to jump through hoops to show that they can care for their children, but sometimes they are frustrated. However, sometimes it might seem like no matter what they do their competence is always being questioned. This can bring a lot of stress in the co-parenting relationship, so please consider what you might be insinuating to the co-parent when you question what goes on during visitation.

Keep the Lines of Communication Open

In toddlers and preschool-aged children, problems can occur because children this age can communicate—but not enough. Parents with children in this age group can prevent a co-parenting disaster, as well as accusations that are made out of overprotective worry and nervousness, by talking about the children between visits and by keeping an open line of communication about bumps, bruises, scraped shins, chipped teeth, shoes that might be too tight and need replacing, and other normal and predictable things that happen to children between two and five years of age.

Compromise, Not Conflict

When you have a choice between compromising and fighting, always opt for compromise. For instance, I have never been a proponent of making a big deal of toilet training, but this aspect of parenting can cause great wars between co-parents during the toddler years. Most frequently the conflict that comes up is Parent A wants to encourage toilet training because the child is going to preschool and the preschool requires it. Parent B does not have the child for that much time, so Parent B does not want to engage in "potty wars." Parent B also wants to show Parent A that she cannot control his life, so if she wants to toilet train, she should do it on her time.

Notice the secondary agenda at work here. The real issue is not toilet training; it is control. Proper toilet training will not determine your child's future mental health. If you really want to protect your child's mental health, ask yourself whether you are making more problems between you and the co-parent than are absolutely necessary. At this age this applies to toilet training, how much junk food your child is allowed to eat, whether your child should be able to sleep in his own bed, whether your child should take a nap in the middle of the day, and whether you promote early reading and other educational skills. Not a single one of these issues is worth fighting over; all of them can be spoken about intelligently and managed with reasonable compromise. In high-conflict cases, they are usually magnified to larger-than-life issues that are harmful to your child and can even ultimately destroy children's mental health. The bottom line is to express your concerns without hysteria and threats so that they will more likely be taken into consideration by the co-parent. If they are not, that is what the courts are there for.

Topic 32
Special Needs of Five- to Eight-Year-Olds

THE PERIOD OF a child's development from five to eight years is a great time to be a parent. Children this age are independent enough to be able to play by themselves and give you some peace and quiet. Many are happy to snuggle and cuddle. They still seek your approval and attention, and they are more compliant than they are during other periods of development. There is probably no better way to ruin this relatively calm parenting stage than to be embroiled in a battle with a disagreeable co-parent.

Make Sure Your Children Feel Secure

For five- to eight-year-olds who do not have the security of stable family, life can be full of anxiety. These are the ages when children start perceiving the finality and sadness of death, which makes them nervous, along with a million other questions that get their little wheels turning. Children begin asking complex questions at this age but do not yet have the advanced thinking skills that can adequately answer the questions. At this age, thinking is still rather black and white.

> **Q**uick Tip: Encourage your child to write, call, or send cards to your co-parent on special days.

Children at this stage will pose many "what-ifs" to themselves, then become very frustrated and anxious if they cannot come up with scenarios that calm the fears the what-ifs bring to their sensitive minds. So they need security. They need to know their parents will be there for them. This means that they need to know that the noncustodial parent will always be there for visitation, and the custodial parent will be at home waiting when they return. It means knowing they can call and speak to the parent they do not live with. It means they want to see Mom's or Dad's face at a soccer practice or a school play. It is not difficult to satisfy those needs when two parents have a cooperative and respectful relationship.

Quick **Tip:** Do not ask your child questions about the other parent's spouse or partner.

When parents do not adequately address the needs of their five- to eight-year-olds, even very relaxed, docile children quickly become cynical and mistrustful; and that is a very bad attribute to produce in a young child, because it only goes downhill from there. Often we hear that children from high-conflict divorces "grow up too fast." When children do not receive the security from their parents they need to grow up healthy, and when they are recruited as soldiers in their parents' conflicts, they feel they have to provide security and reinforcement to their parents. This often comes in the form of expressing loyalty to one parent while criticizing the other, or, worse yet, offering expressions of love to one parent while completely rejecting the other. These are not tasks that young children should be worrying about. They are supposed to get more love than they are required to give out.

Tips for Co-Parenting

Here are some tips for managing the needs of children this age. This advice applies throughout the developmental spectrum but is particularly important in this phase of life.

- Be certain that there is regular contact between both parents.
- Do not make promises you cannot keep. Any promise you make must be seen as a very high priority compared to other

responsibilities that you have. If you say you are going to visit, then visit. If you say you are going to show up at a school event, be there.

- Never cancel your visitation time with your child to go off on a social outing with your new partner and their child.
- Do not force your child to state which parent she likes or loves more.
- Do not criticize your child if he says something positive about the co-parent.
- Do not reject your child if she says she wants to spend more time with the co-parent.
- Do not permit your child to overhear your complaints about the co-parent.
- Do not destroy the co-parent's relationship with teachers, doctors, or other important people in your child's life.

Keeping these courtesies in mind will go a long way in protecting your child's mental health.

Topic 33
Special Needs of Eight- to Twelve-Year-Olds

BEFORE YOU READ this section, it would be a good idea to review the previous section (on the needs of children five to eight years old) because the same general principles apply to this age as well.

Quick Tip: The establishment of a good work ethic can be the single most important coping resource you can teach your child at this and any age.

Co-Parenting Goals

There are three habits every parent of an eight- to twelve-year-old should seek to establish.

- **A good work ethic.** Chores and associated rewards and privileges are an important means of teaching a work ethic.
- **Structured school routines.** Require children to take a brief rest (about an hour) after school and then sit someplace quiet and do their homework.
- **Respect for authority.** Important authority figures include teachers, family members, law enforcement, and the court system. Present a proper model for your children to follow, and allow them to experience the natural consequences of their behavior without bailing them out or making excuses for them.

If you can accomplish these three rather large parenting tasks before your child's teen years, there will be fewer late-night telephone calls to deal with during those teen years.

Work Together to Establish Goals

When you can establish the three aforementioned goals without threats or physical punishment, all while communicating to your children that you love them more than anything, you will likely get a good kid in return for your efforts.

As always, civilized co-parenting and communication buys you a tremendous advantage in influencing the mental health of your child. Be certain to establish common rules on what media content is acceptable, computer use, curfews, the way siblings are treated, homework routines, and responsibilities and chores. It makes a difference in large and small behavioral issues if you do not let your children follow the natural tendency to play one parent off the other.

When You Can't Co-Parent Peacefully

A nasty divorce and a poor co-parenting relationship will defeat your efforts to establish the three goals in the following ways.

Undercutting your child's work ethic. When children grow up in two different homes, it becomes very easy to play one parent off the other. This makes it easy for them to avoid chores and responsibilities on the day of a visitation change because the child knows that Mom and Dad do not talk, so therefore the information that chores are not done will not follow them from Mom's to Dad's or vice versa. This trains children to look for ways to cut corners and avoid work now and in the future.

Undercutting your child's sense of responsibility. The same advice goes for schoolwork. Visits are sometimes rushed and hurried. Children develop convenient memories with respect to what books should come home. Homework is lost, forgotten, or otherwise sucked into the abyss of poor communication between Mom and Dad. The result in the worst cases is failed quizzes, summer school, and parents exchanging blame. In the meantime, there is no lesson to be learned from the child except that "I can keep Mom and Dad more worried about my schoolwork than I have to be, which ultimately leaves me more time to waste time, get myself into trouble, and become a casualty of their divorce." This may sound overly simplistic, but it is exactly how it happens.

> Quick Tip: It's OK to have high expectations of your children even though you and the co-parent are divorced or separated. Research shows that children grow to meet their parents' high expectations as long as there is plenty of love and nurturance in the mix.

Teaching your child the blame game. If you and your co-parent are always pointing fingers—Dad calls the judge a jerk, Mom calls Dad a moron—you give your child the wrong message. Give your child a consistent message that everything is always somebody else's fault, and you can count on your child to learn to cast the blame for everything she does wrong on somebody else: Bad grades are the teacher's fault. A fight is the other kid's fault. If these problems sound familiar to you, it is time to start working with the co-parent and creating a common plan for instilling good work habits, a strong sense of responsibility, and respect for authority.

Topic 34
Special Needs of Teens

As I mentioned in the previous section, there are three essential values that you need to teach your children before they reach age twelve:

- A good work ethic
- Structured school routines
- Respect for authority

Establishing these values and habits is easier said than done. I do not want to give you the impression that any major parenting task occurs without frustration, seemingly endless repeated efforts with long-delayed tangible results, and sleepless nights. Parenting is hard, and it gets harder and requires more creativity during the teen years.

Difficult though it may be, if you do not accomplish these tasks by the time your child reaches his teen years, it might become more difficult to guide him away from trouble—but it is not impossible. The key is communicating. Talk to your teen about everything, even if it appears as though he is not paying attention. The more you talk with your teen, offer your opinion, and avoid peppering him with questions, the more he will talk to you.

Quick Tip: While it is true that teens are strongly influenced by their peers, parental influence doesn't evaporate. Work hard to keep lines of communication open. They are listening, even when they don't seem to be.

The Importance of Cooperative Co-Parenting

The teenage years are the time where children naturally question author-ity and mistrust adults. With good parenting and open lines of commu-nication, parent-child bonds can be strong enough to overcome those difficulties. Consider the teen who has grown up in an atmosphere of hatred, criticism of one parent by the other parent, uncontrolled anger and hostility, indifference, lack of empathy, and failure to offer forgive-ness. That is a long list of negative attributes, but it is these attributes that form and foster conflict between fighting parents. Your children often have no choice but to follow the example you set. How will you overcome your teenager's perception of "do as I say, not as I do" if you tune out the co-parent, refuse to communicate when you are angry, and behave selfishly and without regard for anyone else's feelings? These are the very things we recoil at seeing in our teens. They are the most obnoxious, inelegant aspects of teen life that evaporate even the deepest stores of patience. Yet fighting co-parents demonstrate these behaviors on a daily basis. It is difficult enough to positively influence teenagers when we are not demonstrating the very behavior we seek to eliminate or reduce in them.

Helpful Tips for Co-Parenting Teens

Here are some other suggestions for co-parents who are trying to create fewer problems in their teens.

- **Work with your co-parent to keep track of your teen.** Teens will often let you think they are with the co-parent instead of out partying with their friends. If you communicate with the co-parent, this is one slick move you can nip in the bud.
- **Offer to host.** Whenever you can, allow your teen to hang around with friends at your home, where you can keep track of potential troublemakers and see who is influencing your child.

- **Know that your teen will be supervised when she goes out.** Do not be so quick to permit your teen to disappear to a friend's house for a few days unless you know *for sure* what kind of supervision there is there. If you have been a single parent for a long time, you can get used to your children not being around for periods of time. You will also welcome a break in your parenting chores and an opportunity to socialize or get things done. But letting your child hang out at a friend's house is not like letting her go to the co-parent's for visitation. Stay on top of the details and check up on your kid.
- **Encourage your child to maintain a relationship with your co-parent.** Teens can easily lose track of their relationship with their mother or father. Kids distancing themselves from their parents can happen at any age, but it is particularly problematic during the teen years, when hormones and dramatic thinking can rule their behavior. If your teen decides to cut off his relationship with your co-parent, you must really challenge yourself to push for a reconciliation unless circumstances are extreme. When children align themselves with one parent and reject the other, it can be comforting and validating for the parent the child becomes closer to, but that does not necessarily make it better or healthier for the teen.

Take the case of a father whose teenaged daughter decided never to speak with him again after it was leaked to her that the reason for the divorce was because he was having an affair. While this might be cause for the mother not having a relationship with the child's father, is it a justifiable reason for the daughter not to have one?

One of my observations of children who are going through high-conflict divorces is that they see parents disavowing one another and splitting off from one another on bad terms. This can present a model or example for that behavior. Generally speaking, it is better to have a relationship with an imperfect parent than to have no relationship at all.

Part 5
Making Visitation Schedules Work

Topic 35

Understanding Custody and Visitation in Relation to Parenting Influence and Time

BECAUSE EACH STATE'S laws regarding custody and visitation vary, it is difficult to establish a common set of terms and ideas on these topics. However, from a purely practical point of view, the two items that matter most to parents (and sometimes they do not know this when they are making their own custody agreements) are *influence* and *time*, and these two concepts are important to sort out regardless of where you live.

The concept of time relates to the amount of time and schedule of contact with each parent. Influence usually refers to how parents make important decisions about children and which parent has the right to overrule the other parent's disagreement over how the children should be raised.

There are dozens of combinations of time and influence, and there is rarely only one combination that will benefit kids. While finding a good combination of time and influence is important, obsessing over minutes of contact or complicated protocols for exerting influence can be counterproductive.

To show how different states can vary on the legal definitions of custody, consider New York, the state in which I practice. The court system in New York does not have a statute for "joint custody." The only way you can have joint custody is by agreement; a court cannot order it. Joint custody in New York is whatever two people decide it should be, so the terms of one divorcing couple's joint custody might be very different from the terms of another couple's.

On the one hand, this is a good thing because people's decisions about joint custody are made in an atmosphere of agreement. On the other hand, it creates problems in other areas. For instance, in New York, whoever gets custody also gets child support. So, there are a number of cases where parents are at least equivalent in their ability to raise children, but if one feels the need for that child support check to survive financially, there will be a custody battle.

Texas is a state that does things completely different from New York. In Texas, and many other states, the "default" custody arrangement is joint custody. If people want sole custody they have to sue one another for it.

In Texas they have what is called a *standard possession order*, which describes, among other things, the principles on which children's time should be divided. Notice how directly the Texas Family Code expresses the belief that children should spend quality time with both of their parents:

> *It is the policy of this state to encourage frequent contact between a child and each parent for periods of possession that optimize the development of a close and continuing relationship between each parent and child. It is preferable for all children in a family to be together during periods of possession.*
>
> —Adapted from the Texas Family Code, Sections 153.311 through 153.317

I think what I like best about this section of the law is that it looks to me like it could have been written by a mental health professional!

If You Don't Know, Ask

Do you know your state's policies regarding custody? If you don't, do some research or ask your lawyer. Also ask your lawyer what your state's idiosyncrasies are regarding *residential custody, shared parenting, spheres of influence,* and *alternating weeks.*

Residential Custody

Residential custody is sometimes used to describe whose house a child lives in primarily if there is joint custody but the time is divided disproportionately. The residential custodial parent is often assumed to have more responsibility and influence on day-to-day matters because that is where the child is most.

Shared Parenting

Shared parenting is sometimes used to describe custodial time that is set forth in the form of a plan. Shared parenting plans are usually quite detailed and describe the sharing of time in much more complicated terms than "father visits with the children every other weekend." Shared parenting plans often also describe how much influence or "say" each of the parents has on matters of importance (i.e., formal and religious education, medical decision making, etc.) in the children's lives.

Spheres of Influence

Spheres of influence does not refer to parenting time as much as it applies to decision making and influence. One of the problems with certain kinds of joint custody is that there is no way to break the tie that occurs when parents cannot agree on a decision. Sometimes, in order to prevent this type of stalemate, parents will decide (or a judge will order) that decision-making abilities for major areas will be divided between the parents. The four areas that are often identified for decision making are education, religious training, medical needs, and after-school activities. Dividing influence is a good strategy for making certain that both parents have some say in the decisions that influence their children.

Alternating Weeks

Alternating weeks is more a concept than a term, but it is a term that comes up often enough to warrant discussion. An alternating-week schedule is often an attempt to make certain that both parents have *exactly* the same amount of time. In this type of shared-parenting schedule the children spend one week at their mother's home and then the next week at their father's home, and the schedule alternates like this from week to week. People ask me about this type of schedule more than any other. As with any schedule, there is nothing particularly magical about it. It does offer the advantage of a mathematically equal split of time. I would not recommend a schedule like this for an infant, and certainly not if one of the parents relied heavily on childcare while the other was free to be with the child. I have also noticed that this is not a particularly good schedule when it is forced on people. In terms of influence, it is generally presumed that parents who adopt an alternating-week schedule will also share influence equivalently. Like all schedules, the success of a schedule like this depends a lot on the quality of the co-parenting relationship and how well the children can adjust to it.

Q**uick Tip:** Don't make excessive last-minute demands to change visitation days and times. Everyone has their limits of tolerance.

The next few topics will cover temporary and long-term scheduling and cover different types of parenting plans in detail.

Topic 36
How to Set Up a Temporary Visitation Schedule

ULTIMATELY, WHEN PEOPLE divorce, at some point they will be living in separate residences. This can happen at various different times in the divorce process. It can happen early on because one person moves out or because a judge directs one person to move out. It can also happen later because people decide it is for the best.

When people separate amicably, this is usually a low-conflict circumstance. When people leave out of anger, frustration, or after a physical confrontation, it is a high-conflict circumstance.

At various steps in the divorce process, decisions have to be made as to how, in the short term, children will see both of their parents. Initially, it can be a difficult task, simply because the parents have never contemplated such a split before. Sometimes, one parent does not trust the other parent to manage the children. So, how do parents start dividing the time? For some people it is easy. They have a discussion and agree to divide the time with practical concerns in mind, such as availability or work schedules. For others it's an ongoing battle.

> **Q**uick Tip: Being the custodial parent doesn't give you the right to make decisions that disrupt the co-parent's schedule. Consider the times that your co-parent has visitation to be unchangeable in any way until the co-parent approves.

Assuming that your conflict isn't so out of control that you can't agree that both parents should participate in raising the children, here are some things to think about.

Contact with Both Parents Is Best

In the short term, it is better to give children as much contact as possible with both parents than it is to move right to a rigid visitation schedule. I've heard people respond to this with "But children need structure." Yes, children do need structure, but structure is not as important as maintaining a child's sense of security and reinforcing the belief that even though parents do not live with one another, contact with both parents should be positive and frequent, especially in the initial stages of separation.

The best circumstance I have seen in the short run—between low-conflict, cooperative parents—is where one parent has moved out of the main residence and is allowed to return to help the children with homework or tuck them into bed. This type of familiar contact usually keeps children from going into an immediate panic and can help get them used to a second residence when they start to visit. If a parent can spend some time in the children's main residence as well as having the children spend some time in that parent's new residence, this presents less of a contrast or change in the children's lives and becomes an easier adjustment. This is especially so with children under ten years old.

Immediately after a separation, whenever possible, both parents should try to involve themselves (in a civilized manner) in the children's after-school activities. Children worry that they will be embarrassed by their parents' behavior at sports events, recitals, and dance lessons. Show them from the beginning that they can feel comfortable with both parents attending.

If you are a parent who has not involved yourself in your children's after-school activities, start *now*—just do not make a scene. If you and the co-parent cannot achieve a civilized co-attendance at your children's activities, divide the time and go alone, but understand that this is not the best circumstance for your children.

Quick Tip: Whenever possible, parents should have weekday as well as weekend time with their kids.

Splitting the weekend time is important on a permanent and temporary basis, especially considering the number of two-parent working families. Being a "weekend-only" parent is often not helpful to your relationship with your child or to the co-parent. Both parents should participate in quality parenting time, as well as divide the parenting chores that involve being a chauffeur service, an ATM machine, a coach, and all of the other difficult but necessary facets of parenting.

Some parents divide weekend time by assigning Saturdays to one parent and Sundays to another parent. Sometimes practical aspects such as work schedules dictate that this is the best way to do it, but in most cases it is not practical. Weekend visitation gives one parent an opportunity to involve himself or herself in a block of parenting time that includes bedtime rituals, meals, social activities, and playdates. It also gives the other parent time to catch up on some of the important personal chores that do not involve the children.

On temporary and permanent bases, and for reasons I cannot understand, parents will sometimes abdicate the care of children to babysitters as opposed to the other parent. Sometimes parents do not want to admit that they are not spending their allotted time with the children. Children do tend to report when they are with sitters, so this strategy usually creates more problems than it solves. If you need time alone, you should ask the co-parent to babysit first.

Positive co-parenting requires that you place your needs, desires, and feelings aside and concentrate on your children's needs, desires, and feelings. You might be perfectly happy if you never saw the co-parent again, but always keep in mind that except under rare circumstances, your children probably don't feel the same way.

Topic 37
How to Set Up a Long-Term Visitation Schedule

THIS IS A difficult topic to discuss with people because many myths circulate about how children should share time with their divorced or separated parents. There are certain statements that, when repeated often enough, are taken as facts or standards. The only "fact" that applies to the creation of parenting schedules is that children generally adjust to whatever their parents approve of and feel comfortable with. This means that if two parents decide that an every-other-day visitation schedule, which is typically not a good schedule for children, happens to be what is best for them, the children will most likely adjust; and if they do not adjust, the parents should modify it. Your attitude toward the long-term schedule you choose will determine your children's attitude in most cases.

Making Two Homes for Your Child

There is no visitation schedule that is all good or all bad from a purely practical point of view. You might have to experiment with a few different types of schedules before something will prove to be a good fit in the long term. You will also need to adjust the schedule based on the developmental and social needs of your children.

One very common reason a parent might deny visitation is a stated desire for their children to have "a home base," or "one home." This concern is completely without merit. Most of the time, parents who say they want their children to have a "home base" want to control visitation, or they want to be able to show that they have the children for the majority of time so that they can be awarded child support. It is perfectly normal for children to feel comfortable living in both of their parents' homes.

Quick Tip: There is no compelling research-based evidence that shows kids are better off when they spend the majority of time with one parent for the sole purpose of having a "home base."

With a little work and cooperation, children can have two comfortable beds for sleeping, two places to do their homework, and two parents who act like real parents. The keys to this are cooperation, sharing of parental responsibilities, a common set of disciplinary rules, and civilized behavior between the parents.

When parents live in close proximity, the practical aspects of co-parenting are easier, and it is easier to develop parenting schedules that include sharing weekday time. I do not favor the type of visitation that presumes that the noncustodial parent receives every other weekend visitation and one dinner visit during the week. The typical Wednesday night 6:00 to 8:00 visit rarely amounts to more than the visiting parent running out to a fast-food restaurant, helping the kids do homework on top of greasy wrappers, and running the children back to the custodial parent's home. This becomes even more difficult when the child is involved in an after-school activity like sports or music lessons.

Let's take a close look at the practical aspects of this common visitation schedule. A weekend consists of, at most, Friday evening to Sunday evening, a forty-eight-hour period of contact. If visitation is every other weekend, that makes two forty-eight-hour periods of visitation per month. I typically ask custodial parents if they think two forty-eight-hour periods a month would be enough time for them to influence their child the way they desire. Of course, most say that is not enough, yet many of them find it acceptable for children to have so little contact with the noncustodial parent.

That is because people have been told over the years that this is an acceptable schedule of contact for the noncustodial parent. If the noncustodial parent doesn't want any more time than that, you certainly cannot force it on him. But many parents want to have full and complete relationships with their children. They want to be involved. This cannot happen on an every-other-weekend schedule.

There are several ways to accomplish a more complete relationship between the children and both parents. The first and easiest way is to be certain that the noncustodial parent has access to after-school activities and functions. That way, even if there is only every-other-weekend visitation, the child can see the noncustodial parent during the week in a traditional parenting role. The second way to accomplish this is to permit the noncustodial parent to stop by the children's residence after school to say hello.

This situation might not seem realistic if you and your co-parent hate each other, but the question always boils down to whether you want to do what is best for your children or vent your rage at the co-parent for the rest of your children's lives.

Quick Tip: Don't let your dislike of the co-parent determine your child's need to spend time with her. Visitation is not about you; it is about your children.

When parents cannot tolerate one another's presence, the children should not suffer for lack of contact with either parent. Mom not liking Dad or Dad not liking Mom is not a sufficient reason for denying a child access to a parent. Yet it is the most common reason why visitation is denied or limited.

When Midweek Visits Don't Work

What can a noncustodial parent do when he does not get along with the co-parent and cannot visit the children for practical reasons during the week? One option is to seek more weekend visitation; instead of every

other weekend, try three out of four weekends. Another very successful option is to split the year into ten five-week blocks instead of twelve
four-week blocks. This takes a little more planning, but it can give the
noncustodial parent three out of five weekends instead of two out of
four weekends.

In a three-fifths weekend visitation schedule, the weeks are arranged
in a five-week recurring A-B-B-A-B cycle in which A is the custodial parent and B is the visiting parent. On the first weekend of the cycle, the custodial parent has weekend visitation; on the second and third weekends
the noncustodial parent has the weekend. On the fourth week, the weekend goes to the custodial parent, and on the fifth week, the weekend goes
to the noncustodial parent. After the fifth week, the cycle starts again.

It is best to describe visitation in terms of a repeating cycle rather
than referring to the first week of the month, the second week of the
month, and so on. Months vary in the number of weeks, offering a
cause for confusion and argument over "extra" weekends. Two-week
repeating cycles are adequate to describe most visitation schedules.
When a generic Week 1 and Week 2 are agreed to, simply mark a "1"
or "2" on each Monday of a twelve-month calendar. The entire exercise
takes about two minutes. Make sure that you and the co-parent have
started on the same Week 1.

The Visitation Schedule I Recommend

I am partial to a particular type of shared parenting schedule that I have
seen work well with both high-conflict and low-conflict divorced parents
for many years. I suggest this when both parents are within a twenty-
minute drive to school; when both parents are available to spend most
of the allotted time with the child or children; and when the children
are comfortable and happy with both parents. It is a two-week repeating
schedule.

I will explain it with a notation showing how the children go from
home to home with letters and symbols. The first day always represents
Monday, so that the weekend can be seen as days in a row.

First, designate one parent as A and the other as B. An A in brackets ([A]) means that Parent A has the whole day with the children. A bracketed A/B ([A/B]) means the children go from Parent A to Parent B on that day.

- **Week 1** [A]-[A]-[A]-[A/B]-[B]-[B]-[B/A]. Parent A has the children on Monday, Tuesday, and Wednesday for the entire day. On Thursday, the children go from Parent A to Parent B. They are with Parent B on Thursday after school or in the evening (depending on the transition time). They are with Parent B all day Friday and Saturday, and they return to Parent A on Sunday evening.
- **Week 2** [A]-[A]-[A]-[A/B]-[B]-[B/A]-[A]. Parent A has the children from Monday to Thursday afternoon or evening, just as in Week 1. Instead of the children coming back to Parent A on Sunday, they return on Saturday morning. This is so Parent A can have weekend time with the children.

The advantages to this schedule are numerous.

- **Time is divided equally between the parents.** Parent B gets to see the children on some portion of fourteen out of every twenty-eight days.
- **The children are only out of the Parent A home for six days of every twenty-eight-day period.** Because the children start in Parent A's home on Thursday and spend part of each Sunday or Saturday with Parent A, the children see Parent A for some portion of twenty-two of every twenty-eight days.
- **The children have a regular "transition day" during the school week.** Every Thursday the children go to Parent B's residence. This gives Parent B the opportunity to participate in schoolwork and other activities. Thursday is an important day to prepare for tests and quizzes, so this should satisfy Parent B's

desire to be a "real parent" as opposed to merely a weekend parent.

- **Midweek visitation is eliminated in favor of blocks of parenting time for each parent.** There is no need for rushed visitation, fast-food dinners, or sloppy homework.
- **Because parenting time is distributed in blocks, each parent has "time on" and "time off" with respect to parenting responsibilities.** This is great because when it is each parent's time for parenting, they can concentrate on the children. When it is their "off" parenting time, each parent can tend to their personal responsibilities, their social lives (which should be kept away from the children), and their shopping and personal chores.

There is a single drawback to this schedule: Parent A does not get a "full weekend" with the children, meaning that there is no weekend where Parent A gets to have a Friday night with the children. There is a way to deal with this facet of the schedule. It is called "being reasonable." If Parent A wants to spend a Friday night with the children, she calls Parent B in advance and requests the time. Parent B obliges because Parent B wants the children to do fun things and have fun experiences. Parent A then consents that on the next Week 1 (which is Parent B's longer block of time), Parent B can keep the children on the Sunday night they would ordinarily return and bring them to school on Monday morning so as to make up the missed sleepover.

Be Reasonable

When you are creating schedules, be open-minded. Do not be so quick to count the number of "sleepovers" as being that meaningful. The only useful thing you can do while your kids are sleeping is spend time figuring out how you are going to pay for your lawyer. Consider instead the quantity and quality of face-to-face time you will have with your children. When your children are awake you can tell them how much you love them, and until they are old enough to disappear with their friends and use your residence as a boardinghouse, you can spend your time playing with them and educating them. Those are the important moments, and that is the type of time and contact you should be seeking.

Topic 38
How to Figure Out Holiday Visitation

FIGURING OUT, PLANNING, and successfully executing holiday visitation is a matter of following some simple guidelines.

- Identify which holidays are holidays. (Bastille Day is not a holiday if you and your family have never celebrated it before.)
- Make a list of all the holidays and divide that list into two equal parts.
- Assign one half of the list to one parent and one to the other.
- Alternate those halves of the list from year to year.
- Specify the pick-up and drop-off protocols and times for each of the holidays.

If you can get this far, you will avoid most of the last-minute problems that come up with holiday visitation.

Other Holiday Issues to Keep in Mind

There are some sneaky issues regarding holidays that might not be so easy to anticipate.

Children's Birthdays

There are a few different ways of adding children's birthdays to the visitation calendar. Parents may choose to split the day. This is rarely practical, especially if one parent wants to have a party or the birthday is on a school day. A second option is to have whichever parent does not have the day spend one hour with the child just to wish him a happy birthday. This requires scheduling something extra into a busy day. The third and most practical option is for parents to have separate birthday celebrations with the child on separate days. This works best in high-conflict situations and certainly is not objectionable to the child. In low-conflict situations, and especially with younger children, parents can be civilized enough to have just one party that both attend without ruining the experience for the child.

If you are having trouble with the co-parent, do not keep your child from having some phone contact with the co-parent on the child's birthday. This can give the child the impression that the other parent does not care about him.

> **Q**uick **Tip:** It is best to figure out holiday visitation as early in the year as possible, but be as flexible as you can to make adjustments for special events, such as your co-parent's family coming in from out of town. If that time falls on your side of the schedule, try to be generous and think of the kids.

Please keep in mind that you can only fool kids up to a point. You may try your best to persuade your child that having a relationship with the parent you hate is a waste of time, but children almost always figure out what you are doing, and when they do, it is you they will reject.

Mother's Day and Father's Day

Parents are sometimes tempted to trade weekends on Mother's Day and Father's Day, but it is best to maintain the regular weekend schedule and simply ensure that the children spend Mother's Day with Mom and Father's Day with Dad. For example, if the mother is the custodial parent and Mother's Day falls on Dad's weekend visitation, the child should come back at 10:00 on Sunday morning and spend the day with Mom. If Father's Day does not fall on Dad's weekend, Mom should make them available to Dad for the day (from 10:00 to 8:00 or so).

Legal Holidays

If a legal holiday or some other special time such as summer visitation falls on the same day as regular visitation with the other parent, the legal holiday or summer visitation supersedes the regular visitation. The prime example of this is during summer vacation. Dad is supposed to get two weeks during the summer, but the weekend that falls between the two weeks is Mom's regular weekend visitation. Dad wants to go to Disneyland during those weeks, and Mom says, "Sure, as long as the kids are back in time for my weekend visit," which requires that Dad cut his vacation short by a week. That is not the way it should be done, although I have seen parents try to sabotage visitation enough times to know that this example is in no way far-fetched or unusual. If you think that the co-parent will try to interfere with your visitation or blocks of parenting time, or if you are unclear as to how holidays and vacations are divided, get clarification from your attorney.

Parents' Birthdays

While many adults hate to acknowledge birthdays, they seem to get over this for the purpose of annoying one another with custody and visitation problems. When children attend any family gathering for a parent's birthday, it's usually a good time for the child and certainly a benefit to her. The key here is reciprocation. It must go both ways. If having your child for a portion of time on your birthday is important enough to you, have your attorney put it into your agreement or petition the court at the appropriate time in your legal case.

Halloween

Is Halloween a holiday? Judging by the number of visitation-related fights it inspires, it sure seems to be. The vast majority of Halloween problems occur when children are small and do not mind being dressed up like a turnip or sunflower. Parents sometimes fight over the "right" to take their children trick-or-treating. A good rule of thumb is that if it is fun for your child, and the child has to do it with the other parent, you should be the bigger person and let the child go. Better yet, divide the time and take the child to two fun places.

Summer Vacation and School Recesses

These times should be chosen, scheduled, and agreed to in advance. If the parent with the visitation is planning on taking a trip, she should provide a written itinerary of the trip with complete contact information.

> **Q**uick **Tip:** Try not to transport your kids on "party holidays" when drunk drivers might pose a danger to you and your children on the road.

Holidays That End Late at Night

New Year's Eve and Christmas Eve are two holidays that can end late in the evening. Think twice about scheduling visitation returns late at night on holidays that entail higher risk of drunk-driving accidents. It is better to schedule a return very early the next morning than in the middle of dangerous driving times.

Topic 39
When to Seek
Supervised Visitation

IF YOU FEEL your co-parent is a danger to your children's health and well-being, you can ask the court to require *supervised visitation,* in which the co-parent's visitation is monitored by another person. When supervised visitation is really needed, it can save a child's life. When supervised visitation is not needed, it is one of the most humiliating experiences a parent can go through during a high-conflict divorce or post-divorce action.

Understanding Supervised Visitation

There are instances where parents and children do need to be supervised. Supervised facilities range from those that are watched over by armed guards to those that are more friendly. Information on supervised visitation facilities is usually available through the court. For many years I ran a supervised visitation establishment called The SmartParenting House in a very quaint and comfortable house. Parents visited there and learned good parenting skills in an environment that was an approximation of a natural setting. Parents cooked for their children and learned how to change diapers and do other parenting chores.

Quick Tip: Think carefully about whether you really believe the co-parent requires limited periods of supervised visitation. These will be the memories your child has of his parents growing up.

Everything that happened in the house was recorded on videotape, and there were cameras in every room that relayed images to a supervisor's room. There was usually one social worker at the video bank and one social worker who managed the session.

Each social worker carried panic buttons in case there was a problem. In the tens of thousands of supervised visitation hours I have conducted, there have been very few problems during visitation, and merely a handful of problems in the parking lot. We do not let parents come and go from the same doors in many of my establishments. It is good to look for supervised visitation facilities that keep an eye toward safety.

Supervised visitation time is usually one to two hours per week, so children really do not get that much time to visit with their parents. While my facilities provided cooking facilities, cable television, video games, books, and toys, many establishments do not. Some of the state-run supervised visitation facilities are large auditoriums with long tables that cannot help but remind me of visitation facilities in some of the jails I have worked in. The development of humane and comfortable supervised visitation facilities is something I hope people at each state and community level will take a stronger interest in.

When Supervised Visitation Is Necessary

The circumstances under which supervised visitations should occur are quite varied. Parents who are found guilty of severe abuse (where they have injured a child or sexually molested a child) should not have any visitation at all, but are generally permitted supervised visitation by most courts. Parents who have used poor parenting judgment are often given supervised visitation, but the only effective use of supervised visitation in these cases is when it is combined with a therapeutic and/or educational program that seeks to modify the supervised setting and make the visitation normal again when the parent improves behavior.

Another common reason for supervised visitation is when a parent has recently abused drugs or alcohol. I would say this is a very necessary referral, especially in cases where the abuse has been ongoing. Most twelve-step programs teach clients that they have to accept the natural consequences of their behavior. If you abuse drugs or alcohol, and your co-parent is aware of how potentially dangerous this is to your children, one of those consequences will be a very limited interaction with your children.

When You Obtain Supervised Visitation Unnecessarily

For a moment, let's talk about what happens when you convince the court that supervised visitation is needed when it is not. In other words, before I talk about what life is like from the accused person's side, let me say a few words about parents who seek visitation needlessly as a means of expressing anger or being malicious.

First, when you convince the court that supervised visitation is necessary, you communicate to your child that his parent is a dangerous person who needs to be watched and monitored. This has an effect on the supervised parent's relationship with the children.

Second, you confine your children's childhood memories of the supervised parent to the experience of being in "visitation jail."

Third, you increase the co-parent's motivation to retaliate with legal nonsense that may put you in the same position one day. How does that happen? Judges will order supervised visitation for a parent who "cries wolf." In addition, parents who fake or exaggerate circumstances that lead to unnecessary supervised visitation often lose custody of the children. If you want to play dirty, there are some judges who are slick enough to beat you at your own game, so be warned.

When You Are Sent to Supervised Visitation Unnecessarily

If you are sent to supervised visitation and you do not think this is fair, before your case is taken off the court calendar find out what sort of documentation is required from the visitation facility in order to normalize your contact with your children. You can get "stuck" in supervised visitation if there is no mechanism for you to apply for normal visitation again. My facility will provide an evaluative report for clients, but a report is useless unless you have a court date and a judge to show the evaluation to.

I think it is a good idea for anyone who is sent to supervised visitation to enroll in a parenting course. If you want to show your judge that you are taking the order for supervised visitation seriously, this is the best way to do it.

It is a bad idea to make a pain in the neck of yourself at the supervised facility, even if you feel as though you have been sent there unfairly. The people who run the facility had nothing to do with sending you there, in most instances. Good facilities provide you with a list of rules you must follow prior to beginning your supervised visitation. Many people going through high-conflict custody make things worse for themselves than they already are. This happens because they feel frustrated, picked on, abused, and taken advantage of. Yes, all of these things happen, and sometimes despite the system's best efforts, they happen unfairly. There is no point in defeating your own best interests, however. Patience and civilized behavior will generally get you to the end of most court-related problems.

Part 6
Dealing with Common Problems

Topic 40
When Parents Have Different Rules

CONSIDER THESE SITUATIONS: Mom does not object to her sixteen-year-old daughter getting a belly button ring, but Dad threatens to pack the teen up and send her to a convent if she does. Eight-year-old Tommy can stay up to watch wrestling on weekend visitation with Dad, but Mom restricts Tommy's television, puts him to bed earlier than Dad, and will not permit him to watch people flinging each other around and dropping them on their heads.

There are three major problems parents create when they do not agree on a common set of rules or limitations on their children.

Quick **Tip:** Do not allow behavior that you know the other parent disapproves of. If you feel that it is absolutely necessary to go against the co-parent, tell the co-parent first; don't let the child bring the news home.

- **Children will divide and conquer.** Children of divorced parents have a natural tendency to divide and conquer, which they will develop with increasing expertise as time goes on. Soon your child will convince you that the other parent has given permission for things when she has not, and you will be raising a child who is growing up to lie and manipulate.
- **Children choose leniency.** When children encounter a choice that doesn't involve consulting either parent (for instance, "Should I smoke this joint?"), the child, having had an experience with one parent who is more lenient (it doesn't have to even be the same parent every time), will choose the less

responsible option. That is because the child is accustomed to having a less responsible or strict option.

- **Disobedience is reinforced.** When children can "cancel" one rule from one parent with permission from another parent, children are reinforced for being disobedient. This ultimately makes it easier for them to be disobedient to both parents.

Quick **Tip:** Do not encourage your child to bring pets or other living things home to the other parent's house without asking first.

Imagine what you would do if you worked for two bosses, each of whom had equal power over you but for much of the time disagreed as to what your job responsibilities and expectations were. Assume that for all of your job tasks, one boss or the other would always require more work of you. It would not take long for you to figure out how to interact with those bosses in such a way as to keep your job but actually work as little as possible given the choices each would present. It would also be a very difficult environment for you to work in because you would always be annoyed at one of your bosses.

How to Agree on One Set of Rules

If there is an area of co-parenting that requires making concessions and really working with the co-parent, this is it. Even if you have only an ounce of patience with your co-parent, dedicate it here. Sit down with your co-parent (and, if necessary, a neutral third party) and have a comprehensive face-to-face discussion about behavioral dos and don'ts for your children. Know what you are going to discuss, make a list, and go through each item. Be prepared to compromise here and there for the sake of creating a well-defined list of rules and consequences. There is room for variation on things like bedtimes and curfews, as long as the variations are minor, like a 9:00 bedtime at one parent's home and an 8:30 bedtime at the other's.

Quick Tip: Both parents' rules can be similar (in other words, they don't have to be equal to the letter), but they should be equivalently strict, or your children are going to learn how to take advantage of the differences.

When You Can't Agree on One Set of Rules

Regardless of how important you think it is to have a common set of goals and rules, the other parent may refuse to enforce them. The inevitable outcome is that if you are the stricter of the two parents, your child will complain that you are unfair, unreasonable, unlikable, and unsympathetic. Parents often feel that the best way of replying to these complaints is by saying something sarcastic like "I'm sorry if your mother [father] doesn't care about the way you grow up. I do, so when you are here you will do it my way."

Instead, try being sympathetic to the fact that the child is getting mixed signals from you and the co-parent. You can say something like this instead: "I don't blame you for being annoyed at the fact that you have to live by two different sets of rules. I would feel the same way. I will try to consider what you think is fair, but I can't always agree. When you are at your mother's [father's], you might be permitted to do things you cannot do in this house. I have to try to set the rules that I think are best for you when you are here, because when you are here you are my responsibility, and I have to set down the rules that I am comfortable with."

Sometimes when we give messages to our children, the most important ones do not sink in right away but still have a profoundly positive influence on the way they grow up. What I am recommending is that you acknowledge your child's feelings and concentrate on your role as a caregiver. Your child may continue to complain, but he will be forced to try to understand your position, as you have demonstrated that you understand your child's position.

Better still, avoid having to deal with this conflict at all by making every attempt to get on the same page as your co-parent and cooperatively disciplining your children.

Topic 41
Discipline Problems Related to Divorce

CHILDREN CAN HAVE discipline difficulties related to their parent's divorce that show themselves in three major ways.

- **Preexisting problems get worse.** Preexisting or long-standing discipline problems that are not necessarily related to divorce are made worse by the divorce or separation.
- **Children act out.** Children are angry, disappointed, frustrated, or conflicted by aspects of their parents' divorce and therefore tend to act out.
- **Children learn negative behavior.** Children watch how their parents behave toward one another, and can in this way learn to be rude, insensitive, hostile, physically violent, disrespectful, and argumentative, to name only a few problem behaviors.

Let's look at each of these discipline problems a bit more closely.

Preexisting Problems

Preexisting problems may exist because a child has a very difficult-to-manage behavioral style or temperament. There are some children who are predisposed to behavioral problems that arise from stubbornness, noncompliance, or aggressiveness in their genetic makeup. It is important for parents to know that their children are difficult and require specialized parenting techniques as opposed to simply blaming the divorce or blaming one another.

It is especially important for parents to cooperate in seeking appropriate intervention from counselors and therapists who specialize in this type of parenting. Preexisting problems are often made much worse by parenting conflicts. Difficulties related to the child erode the co-parenting relationship, while difficulties in the co-parenting relationship worsen the child's behavioral problems. Reducing these conflicts can improve both parents' ability to manage difficult behavior in children. High-conflict parents must choose whether it is more important to keep trying to get back at the other parent or to try to improve the behavior and ultimate success of their difficult child.

Acting Out

Sometimes the divorce is the sole issue that creates the foundation for most, if not all, of a child's disciplinary problems, as well as problems such as anxiety and depression. Children of divorced parents often discover that their disciplinary problems are the only things that bring their parents into the same room or same house to talk. This can reinforce the child's fantasy that Mom and Dad will get together again. The best way to approach this situation is to seek family counseling, in which this dynamic is likely to come to light.

If you are in this situation, you and your co-parent must do your best to communicate that you will always work as a team to make sure the children are healthy and happy, but that does not mean you will get back together. Some children have a difficult time forgiving their parents for separating. This can happen even when parents have a cordial relationship with one another, because it is difficult for kids to understand why people who can be nice to one another could not remain together.

Quick **Tip:** Kids will act out as a way of trying to bring their parents back together. If you think this is the case, sit down with your children and tell them that their acting out will not bring you together—it will just make each one of you worry about them more.

Negative Learned Behavior

By far, the worst influence on a child's behavior (which then affects parents' ability to control and manage that behavior) is the behavior parents model when they engage in a high-conflict relationship. Children imitate not only specific behaviors of their parents, but the style in which their parents treat others. Children also repeat aspects of their parents' behavior toward one another in their friendships and early dating relationships. If you and the co-parent curse each other and call each other names, do not be surprised when your child does the same to you when you displease her. If you and the co-parent are aggressive to one another, do not be shocked when your children are rough or violent with one another. If you end your arguments by storming out of the room and slamming the door, ask yourself what good it does to punish a child for ignoring you and walking away from your reprimands, after seeing the way you handle your difficulties.

In all of these cases, you would do best to join a divorced parenting discussion group, read more books on divorced parenting, or consult a professional.

Topic 42
Preventing Common Personal and Social Problems Related to Divorce

CHILDREN WHO GROW up with divorced or separated parents are subject to a number of disruptions in their personal and social lives, including the following:

- If Mom and Dad do not live close by, participation in organized sports or after-school activities may be difficult.
- Shy children may have a difficult time making two sets of friends.
- Children from high-conflict divorce may gravitate to dysfunctional peer groups, where acceptance into the peer group relies on the child's participation in activities that may involve the consumption of drugs or alcohol, or may involve criminal activities such as stealing or gang violence.
- Children from high-conflict divorce may suffer from problems with self-esteem. This can have disastrous consequences to young girls, who may feel they have to engage in sexual activities to gain acceptance from boys. It can also take the form of alcohol and drug abuse, aggression, delinquency, eating disorders, and a host of other problems.
- Children from high-conflict divorce may have a difficult time learning normal and healthy interpersonal skills because of the example their parents set. As a result they may have trouble making and keeping relationships with friends.

These problems are worsened by the fact that when parents are adjusting to the stresses and strains of single parenting, their children may not be supervised or monitored as closely as they should be. For instance, if your thirteen-year-old daughter tells you she is going over to a friend's house on a night that you are dying for a few hours to yourself, you might be less prone to check up on what she is doing.

To overcome these easy-to-make mistakes you must be extra diligent about what your children are doing and with whom. It is always a good idea to permit your preteen and teenaged children to spend some time with their friends around the house because that will give you the opportunity to meet their friends and see who they are hanging out with. Also, have a conversation with the parents of any child that your child spends a lot of time with or at whose house your child sleeps over.

> **Q**uick **Tip:** It might be harder as a single parent, but as kids get older you have to stay sharp as to what kind of media they are tuned into and what they are viewing and publishing on the Internet.

Also, be sure to monitor your children's media activities. You should develop rules about what is acceptable to watch and set limits on cell phone and computer activities. Make sure computers are used in open areas of the living space. Develop rules about websites that are off limits. For younger children or children who have broken the rules before, be certain that you know what pictures, videos, and media are being uploaded and downloaded.

As I have mentioned before, the single most important thing you can do as a parent is talk to your children and listen to them when they talk to you. It seems like a ridiculously simple piece of advice to follow, but it is an important one.

Finally, keep your kids busy with after-school activities that stress positive values. Your child's sports and extracurricular participation does not have to be eliminated because parents live an inconvenient distance from one another. If you have to drive to get your child to his sports practices and games, your child should not be deprived of the experience merely because it is inconvenient to you. Also, many coaches are very tolerant and flexible about a child who must go back and forth on alternate weekends for visitation, and are willing to make exceptions to rules about making every practice and game in order to stay active on the team.

Topic 43
Preventing Academic Problems Related to Divorce

MOST OF CHILDREN'S academic problems that are related to divorce occur because parents are challenged by the difficulties of post-divorce life and cannot stay on top of their children's schoolwork. This is especially so when single parents work, when they have to rely on childcare and babysitters, and when the children discover that it is easy to get away with not doing homework because Mom or Dad is too tired to check it.

Academic problems require quick identification and immediate action. Keep in regular contact with your children's teachers. You may wonder how much of your family difficulty you should describe to teachers. I would say not much. Teachers know that children have adjustment difficulties related to parental separation and divorce. All any teacher needs to know is that your child may be experiencing some adjustment difficulties because you are separating or divorcing, and that you would like to know what you can do at home to help the teacher at school.

If your child is having trouble in school, first refer the child to the school's child study team to determine whether the difficulties are related to learning problems or motivational and behavioral problems. Also, request that the child's intellectual potential and achievement be tested. You can ask the classroom teacher. If your school does not have the facilities to test your child, make arrangements to have the child tested outside of school.

Intelligence tests provide feedback on the intellectual potential of the child, indicating whether intelligence is above average, average, or below average. A child who has average intelligence should be able to do average work in an average classroom of his peers.

Achievement tests will provide feedback on whether your child is at, above, or below grade level in the main academic areas, such as reading, math, and science.

Quick Tip: If you are unsure as to whether your children's academic needs are being met, request a meeting with the teachers and ask for an evaluation.

Learning Disabilities

If intelligence is at least average, and achievement tests show that your child's achievement is significantly (usually half the expected level) below average, that is a common definition of a learning disability. Children who have learning disabilities show a discrepancy between what their potential is and what they have actually achieved. If your child has a learning disability, your school may have a program that can design an individual education plan to address his particular learning problems.

Emotional Problems

Sometimes emotional problems can cause a decline in achievement. If your child is at least average in intelligence and does not have a learning disability, you and your co-parent should look at two possible problems: homework avoidance and depression.

Homework avoidance. Homework avoidance is when your child develops a pattern of avoiding homework that ultimately leads to a decline in academic performance. Many school subjects, such as math, build one skill on top of the next. If a child starts to avoid homework and does not reinforce skills, it is likely that she will never catch up and will continue to fall behind.

Some children do not like school and will not do homework because they would rather do something more entertaining after school, like play video games or go outside with friends. To help your child live up to his academic potential, structure your child's time after school, and keep on your child to get it done.

One mistake that parents make is to let homework avoidance go too long before doing anything about it. Homework problems tend to follow children year to year. The first time parents discover that their child is avoiding homework, they should keep in regular touch with teachers and step up their own supervisory efforts, requesting regular progress reports to make certain that the child is not lying about homework assignments.

When children and parents are locked into a struggle over homework, co-parents must put their heads together and cooperate on how to get the child back on track. It is counterproductive when one of the parents refuses to crack down on the child because that parent sees the child less often and doesn't want to spend his visitation time scolding the child over homework or being the homework monitor. But just because you see your child for less time, that doesn't reduce your share of parenting responsibility.

Parents who do not see their children often complain that they are not allowed to have full and complete relationships with the children. Having a full and complete relationship with the children includes teaching them to be productive members of society and responsible adults. The way you teach children how to be responsible is by teaching them to honor their commitments. Homework is a commitment, so start teaching.

Depression. Childhood depression is a serious problem for children of divorce. It can cause children to withdraw from peers and after-school activities and lose interest in school and homework. Childhood depression can be identified by a loss of energy, lack of interest in normal childhood activities like playing with friends, frequent crying, sad mood, and making statements such as "I want to be dead." If you see these signs in your children, please cooperate with the co-parent in taking your child to see a qualified mental health professional who specializes in children.

Topic 44
Visitation Tantrums

CHILDREN THROW TEMPER tantrums over visitation for a number of reasons, so it is unwise to assume that the "real reason" is because he is not well taken care of at the other parent's home.

Quick **Tip:** Children rarely refuse visitation when they are given lots of prompting and advance preparation. Prepare the children well in advance by speaking positively about it.

Reasons Children Don't Want to Visit

Some of the reasons children give for not wanting to visit with the other parent include the following:

- "It's boring."
- "I don't like the other people there."
- "I am afraid to sleep over."
- "I am left with a babysitter while Mom [Dad] goes out."
- "I don't like the food."
- "I get hit when I am there."
- "Dad [Mom] likes [somebody else] more than they like me."

There may be other reasons, but these statements cover most of them. When a child's protests are exaggerated and seemingly just whining, the issue usually boils down to these reasons:

- I don't want to leave my main house, which is comfortable and has all my stuff in it.
- I am not getting enough attention, and I don't like sharing attention.

When the protests are not exaggerated there may be a true cause for concern because the child may be saying she is being neglected, ignored, or abused.

Attending to Your Child's Concerns

To properly attend to your child's concerns, speak with her in a neutral way, and try not to make any assumptions. Ask your child to tell you what a typical visit is like. If your child complains of being hit or spanked, ask him to tell you a story from the beginning of what was happening before the spanking to what happened after the spanking. Be aware that children will often exaggerate the negatives of what happens when with the visiting parent, especially if negatives are what seem to get the most attention from you. (A parent's getting excited and hysterical can be very rewarding for children because it teaches them how important they are when they are giving bad news about the other parent.)

Encourage Visitation

When you see cranky behavior before visitation, do your best for the first few visits to encourage visitation. One of the worst ways to encourage a child to go to visitation is to give the child a rest or break from visiting. When this happens, the child often knows she is disappointing the other parent, and she feels even more nervous and guilty the next time it is time to visit. As a result, she might protest even more. The parent the child is with more often can make the situation worse by starting arguments with the co-parent and making the child feel bad about not visiting.

Talk to Your Co-Parent

Before you even think about cutting off visitation, do your best to have a conversation with the co-parent. Begin your conversation with the following: "I have been having a rough time getting Judy to go to visitation. Can you tell me how she is in the car and once she gets there?" This will make the co-parent less defensive because it implies that you are willing to accept that once the child leaves the house she is fine. Don't expect any gentle prodding to be taken well by a co-parent who has a hostile relationship with you. This type of problem solving is simply impossible when parents do not have a good relationship—just one more reason why it is so important to try to maintain a good relationship.

Get Professional Help

If the child starts to regularly complain, it is time to enlist the aid of a counselor who is familiar with this problem. Invite the co-parent to participate from the first session so that the co-parent does not feel as though the counselor is simply your ally. A good counselor should be able to get to the bottom of the child's complaints.

When parents have a good relationship with one another, they can sit down with the child together and ask what would make visitation happier. Often, children do not know, so if this approach does not yield something practical, do not push it. Frequently, children do not want to be interrupted playing, or they do not value time with the other parent. This occurs when parents divorce when children are very young and children do not have a good model of the give-and-take that is required in relationships.

At some point, children will refuse visitation because there is not enough in it for them. They reject visitation because they are not properly entertained. This can be the case where one parent has the means to take them to the movies, shopping, and out to eat on a regular basis, and the other parent does not. When this is the case, parents need to work on teaching the child that a person's company is just as important as the amount of rides they will take you on. By the same token, visiting parents must stimulate their children. Your six-year-old might become very bored sitting next to you on the couch while you watch football games on Sunday.

Also, children will tune into your moods and react accordingly. If you are sad, lonely, or depressed, and this is what your child sees during visitation, eventually he might not want to be in your company. If this is the case, it is time to seek some counseling for yourself.

When Your Child Wants to Live with the Co-Parent

Children will also tell you that not only do they want to go to the other parent's house, they also want to live there.

What Not to Say

First, I will tell you what not to do. Do not say any of the following:

- "OK, pack your stuff and call your father [mother]—you can leave right now."
- "Never. As long as I am alive you will not live with that moron. You are here, like it or not."
- "Sure. Go where life is easy and it's playtime all the time. Take the easy way while I sit here and rot."
- "Shut your mouth and go to your room. I never want to hear you say anything like that again."

Assuming that your child is not chronically unhappy, and that she is telling you she wants to live with the other parent primarily to push your buttons, what your child is really saying is that she is angry, bored, or otherwise irritable. Now consider this: when you are angry, bored, or otherwise irritable and someone says something nasty or confrontational to you, how do you respond? You probably get angrier and crankier, if you are like most people.

Parents do not have endless patience, but children often appear as though they have an endless capacity to twist parents' guts. Eventually something snaps, and you are at war with your child. This happens most when parents need something their children do not want to give, like cooperation, and when children want something their parents do not want to give, like expensive new shoes.

Children from divorced homes naturally conclude that there are two venues available, and when one parent does not give what they want, the other parent might. Heck, it can't hurt to ask.

One thing you never want to do when a child has a tantrum and says she wants to move is to throw a tantrum yourself. The only thing you will accomplish by doing this is to teach your child what she needs to do whenever she wants to make you lose control. Bite your tongue, take ten deep breaths, walk out of the room if you have to, but do not let "I want to live with . . ." become "magic words."

What to Do

This is not a situation that always requires a conversation with the co-parent. Often, it doesn't even require much of a conversation with a child. You can say, "I am sorry you are so unhappy. The decision regarding where you live is an adult decision, and even though you probably don't like hearing it, you do not get to choose that."

Your child may ask you whether he will ever get to choose, and the answer would be either yes or no, depending on what you have discussed with the co-parent or other factors. Whatever the answer is, be firm and decisive and follow up with, "I wish I could do all of the things that make you happy and comfortable here, and I will listen to you tell me what I can do to make you happy here. Saying you want to live someplace else is difficult for me to listen to, but if that is the way you feel, that's OK. Let's try to talk about the things that we might be able to change. I am sorry I can't talk to you about the things we can't change, like where you will live."

Statements like these are meant to initiate a dialogue with your child. That is not always possible. You might want to consider trying again when your child calms down a little.

When Your Child Is a Teen

When children get into their teen years, they often say they want to live with the other parent because the grass might seem greener on that other side. It will not be as easy to be decisive and firm with teenagers, because teens react to this by engaging you in discussions about their rights, freedoms, privileges, and whatever else they can come up with. You might want to consider offering your child the opportunity to spend more time with the other parent if that is what he seems to be asking for.

If your teen wants to go to the other parent's house because her school grades are slipping and you are requiring her to be responsible and clean up her act, engage your child in a discussion that encourages her to ask you again when her grades have improved. If your child's performance is slipping in school, it might be worth changing the visitation schedule or even the living arrangements if nothing else has worked to motivate him to improve. By the time children reach teen years, they have precious few years left before they are out of the house and on their own. You would be doing them a favor in more ways than one if you can help them be prepared for college.

As with most parenting choices and decisions, it is helpful to have a good relationship with the co-parent. Both of you should give your child the consistent message that before any changes are made, grades must improve. You don't want the decision to change living arrangements to reinforce your child's desire to escape responsibility; furthermore, it's possible that the co-parent will not properly supervise the child, in which case the change could prove disastrous. Every case has its own set of circumstances. Cooperating with the co-parent in finding a solution that motivates your child to perform closer to her potential is a good parenting choice, but it is only available when divorced parents try to get along.

When You are the Noncustodial Parent

If you are the noncustodial parent, it will probably happen at some point that your child tells you that she does not want to leave to go back to the other parent's home. If a child is young enough when two parents divorce, this will most likely occur on a regular basis. When it does happen, do not be so quick to assume that it is because your child is chronically unhappy or mistreated. If your child loves both of you, she will be sad when she has to leave either of you. This is especially true of younger children, who think and behave in more concrete terms and are more likely to fuss about leaving because the act of leaving makes them upset and the thought of not leaving would make those bad feelings go away (in their world).

I often hear from visiting parents that young children have a difficult time leaving, and they protest when it is time to go. I also hear from the custodial parents in these cases that the same child cries and protests when visitation time comes and they have to leave.

As children get older and more verbal, they might talk about being unhappy at their main residence. As you are listening to the child complain, you must make a very difficult evaluation: Do you think your child is complaining because the act of complaining brings lots of attention from you? Or, do you think your child is genuinely communicating discomfort in the custodial parent's house? If you do not have an open line of communication with the co-parent, or if your relationship with the co-parent is hostile and combative, it will be very difficult for you to make an honest assessment of what is going on.

You might want to consider the opinion of a professional counselor who works with children of divorced parents, but when you do, it would be best to invite the other parent to participate from the very beginning. In the best-case scenario, the counselor might be able to give you and the co-parent some reasonable suggestions on how to make your child feel more comfortable in her situation. If you decide that the current situation is not in the best interests of your child and believe that you need the court to intervene to change it, you will be taken far more seriously if you can show that you tried your best to use counseling as a form of problem solving before seeking legal relief.

Part 7
Special Concerns and Crisis Situations

Topic 45
When Your Co-Parent Abuses Drugs or Alcohol

DRUG AND ALCOHOL abuse is a factor that impairs a parent's ability to manage children effectively. In the worst situations, drug and alcohol abuse can threaten the safety and lives of your children.

Handling Allegations of Drug and Alcohol Abuse

Handling allegations of drug and alcohol abuse can be very difficult within the context of high-conflict co-parenting relationships. One parent complains that the other is abusing drugs or alcohol, and the other parent complains that the allegation is baseless and is being used as an excuse to gain custody or restrict visitation.

Other factors can further complicate the issue of drug or alcohol abuse.

- The person making the allegation might have enabled the drug or alcohol abuse in the past, or assisted in hiding it from other family members.
- The person being accused might be abusing a substance, but no evidence (such as a treatment record or convictions) exists to prove the abuse in court.
- The diagnosis of drug or alcohol abuse is evaluated in clinical settings using information supplied by family members. In a legal setting, this diagnosis is thought to be mitigated by the fact that allegations are sometimes exaggerations of real events, or outright lies, so evaluators often do not know whom to believe.

Most courts I have worked in are neither sympathetic to nor skeptical of people making allegations of drug abuse. Many judges handle an allegation of substance abuse by referring the alleged abuser for drug or alcohol testing, just to be conservative.

Drug and Alcohol Testing

The process of testing for drugs and alcohol is not perfect. Alcohol testing is effective only for relatively short "look-back" periods. Most alcohol tests cannot accurately detect whether someone has consumed alcohol to excess unless the test happens to occur on a day that the subject has consumed to excess.

Drug tests usually test either urine or hair. Urine tests are not foolproof and can be "beaten" in many different ways. As a rule of thumb, pot, cocaine, amphetamines, painkillers, and barbiturates can be detected for one to three days after use. If someone is a heavy, daily user of pot, use can be detected (though not always reliably) for up to thirty days. Many drug screening facilities now have sophisticated technology that helps identify when someone tries to hide the presence of drugs in their bodies.

Urine tests can be unreliable in detecting many types of abuse in many situations. Drug tests that test hair can look back for three, six, twelve, or even more months, depending on the length of the hair. Many judges will order people to have hair tests and simultaneously order that the person tested not cut, process, or color the hair. Some judges require that a Polaroid picture be taken of the person sent for drug testing so that there is a record of the length of the person's hair from court date to court date.

If you are encouraging your attorney to have the judge order a drug test, have a list of acceptable facilities ready to give the judge. Do not accept hair testing by Internet companies that say they offer the testing when someone mails a sample of hair to them. There is no way of knowing whose hair is being sent for testing. Make sure the facility you use for drug testing does a photo ID check of the person you are sending for testing. Sometimes people will send impostors to give a sample if the ID procedure is sloppy.

Hair tests can be expensive. I have seen the prices for hair testing range from $250 to $2,000. Before sending anyone to a facility, check to see whether the director of the facility has given expert testimony regarding the results of the tests and their accuracy. You would not want to spend a substantial amount of money only to have the tests not accepted as evidence or successfully refuted by the opposing attorney.

Giving Compelling Testimony

If you cannot prove drug or alcohol abuse by a person's history or by drug testing results, you will have to prove it on credibility: your word against the word of the accused, as evaluated by a judge. The most compelling testimony is the most specific. That means you must carefully and meticulously document times, dates, and places where you suspect the co-parent was high or drunk. It's helpful to offer witnesses to back up your story if you can.

Be prepared for some very difficult questions about your own behavior while this investigation is going on. For instance, if you ever left your children alone with the person you now say is abusing drugs and alcohol, you will have to face the possibility that you are credible with respect to your allegations of abuse but guilty of neglecting your children's safety.

When You Are Falsely Accused

Suppose you are being accused of drug or alcohol abuse and you believe that the allegation is false and malicious. The first thing to bring to everyone's attention is information related to the following:

- Traffic-related incidents involving drugs or alcohol
- Results of drug tests required by employers
- History of alcohol- or drug-related problems at work

- History of drug or alcohol treatment or hospitalization
- Family history of drug or alcohol abuse
- Criminal history related to drugs or alcohol

If there is no evidence against you in any of the areas listed, volunteer to take drug or alcohol tests immediately and offer to provide the results directly to the co-parent's attorney through your attorney. If you want to communicate strongly to the court that you do not have an alcohol problem, offer to consent to refrain from the use of any alcohol during your contact with the children.

If none of this is satisfactory to the co-parent, the co-parent's attorney, or the court, the allegation will have to be examined by a judge at a trial, hearing, or other legal proceeding in which you will have to give testimony about your drug or alcohol history. If that is the case, a judge will evaluate your honesty and the co-parent's honesty and make a decision based on those perceptions.

Topic 46
Protecting Yourself and Your Children Against Violence in the Family

FAMILY VIOLENCE IS a massive problem in our country. This includes men being violent against women, women being violent against men, men and women being violent against children, and children being violent to their parents and grandparents.

Quick Tip: Pushing, tapping on the shoulder, poking, and other kinds of touching during an argument will be called "abuse," whether you think it's abuse or not. Think twice about touching the co-parent in any way, and remember that jail is not a fun place.

Understanding Domestic Violence

Family stress increases the potential for violence. Violence often escalates in a predictable pattern that goes from arguing, to cursing, to screaming, to pushing, to punching and kicking, to severely injuring, and then to murder. There is sometimes a family violence component associated with high-conflict divorce. The most important piece of advice I could give to anyone living with violence or abuse is to get help. Tell your story to a counselor, a lawyer, a minister, or a close friend. You can call the National Domestic Violence Hotline twenty-four hours a day, seven days a week, at 1-800-799-7233.

Emotional Abuse

Quick Tip: Saying things like "I'm going to kill you" can earn you a night in jail, even if you've never so much as swatted a gnat. Say less, not more, during an argument.

Some forms of abusive behavior do not involve physically striking someone but can be just as painful and damaging psychologically. Emotionally abusive behavior includes the following:

- Bullying
- Constantly criticizing
- Daily name calling and cursing
- Demeaning the co-parent in front of the children
- Encouraging the children to demean the co-parent
- Encouraging the children to view the co-parent negatively
- Demeaning the children

Quick Tip: If you are not certain that you can control your temper during your contact with the co-parent, bring someone who can help keep you in line. Do not bring anyone who will egg you on to do something stupid.

Physical Abuse

A single push, shove, or slap is a sign that there is something terribly wrong in any intimate relationship. The moment that single push, shove, or slap is ignored, the relationship goes from bad to worse. You will hear no fancy psychological talk or theorizing about this topic. In my mind, it is very cut-and-dried. By the time a relationship becomes physical in any way, the lives of the participants are in jeopardy.

I present this topic in such black-and-white terms because I have seen what happens when family violence is allowed to escalate.

I have evaluated family homicides, attempted murders, ritualistic beatings and torturing of children, marital rape, and horrific emotional abuse in hundreds of cases. The perpetrators of violent family crimes have been men, women, and children. The victims have been men, women, and children.

The extent to which the judicial system will "believe" allegations of abuse varies tremendously. Some courts protect the alleged victim even when it is clear that the story is completely fabricated; some ignore indisputable signs of abuse and violence. There is no guarantee that one who has been abused will be believed, and no guarantee that one will be found innocent of abuse allegations that are based on lies and misrepresentations. That is not because the judicial system is crooked or dishonest, but simply because the skills that even the most competent human beings have for evaluating the truth in these cases are faulty and unreliable.

You must do everything in your power to protect your own safety and the safety of your children, but remember that if you are behaving out of spite and malice and are not abused but say you are, you are risking losing custody of your children in the process.

How to Protect Yourself

Quick **Tip:** Watch the physical space between you and your co-parent when you are talking. Close proximity during heated conversations is threatening.

You can increase the odds of protecting your own safety (and the safety of the children) by doing the following:

- Learn how to de-escalate conflict.
- If you cannot de-escalate conflict, take a break and leave a tense and conflict-ridden situation when you can.
- Start talking to a counselor or therapist sooner rather than later. There are a number of good reasons for this. The first

is that most counselors and therapists who deal with violence and abuse will tell you to start making plans to get out of the environment you are in, and sometimes that means getting out of the house. I believe that people need to hear statements like this often and from as many people as possible until they finally act on it. Start putting yourself in a position where you will hear it.

Another reason to talk to a counselor or therapist is that someone will be making a record of what you are complaining about close to the point in time that you are being mistreated. If the time ever comes that you will need to prove a history of violence or abuse, it is more credible when there is a record of something that is consistent with the point in time that you are claiming abuse. (This is in contrast to the person who goes to a therapist or counselor after an allegation of abuse has been made and starts complaining about what happened six months ago.)

- Try to get the person you are in conflict with to go to therapy with you. This can not only help defuse the situation but also give someone outside the relationship an opportunity to look at both of you in a neutral and impartial manner. If your co-parent resists, do not force the issue. If you are too threatened or intimidated, don't go.
- When a victim wants to leave an abusive environment, lack of funds is often what prevents leaving the environment. If you need protection from abuse, start saving money as soon as possible. Set aside some credit on credit cards; borrow from family members, if necessary. Consider financial sacrifices a matter of survival.
- Develop safety strategies that help you reach out in an emergency. Keep a close friend's or relative's number on your speed dial. Create a code word or phrase that you can use with a trusted person to advise the person to call the police to your house when there is an emergency.

- Get information from reliable, reputable hotlines and informational sources. See the Resources section in the back of the book for a list of domestic violence organizations that can help.
- If your child is being abused, call the child abuse hotline in your area. These telephone numbers are listed in every public telephone book. You can make an anonymous call, but assume that if the person you are reporting lives with you, you may be putting yourself at risk.
- If you have to flee the home, try to communicate with someone who knows the abuser that you are leaving and that it is not your intent to deny the person access to the children, but that you are being physically hurt or threatened and you are in fear of your and your children's health and safety.

Topic 47
What to Do When the Other Parent Speaks Negatively About You to Your Child

ONE OF THE most destructive things you can do to your own relationship with your child is to speak negatively about the other parent in front of your child. Assuming for the moment that you have a very good reason to dislike the co-parent, you nevertheless should have a selfish interest in not bad-mouthing the other parent in front of your child.

> **Quick Tip:** As a general rule, the fewer questions you ask a child, the more the child will tell you.

Why Bad-Mouthing Is Never a Good Idea

Speaking negatively about the other parent demonstrates hatred, and children learn what their parents demonstrate. Expressing your anger toward your co-parent in front of your child is likely to destroy positive perceptions your child has about the co-parent.

> **Quick Tip:** Do not quiz your children about what they ate at the co-parent's house. If you think your child is being deprived of proper nutrition, speak to the co-parent directly.

However, it rarely stops there. When your child gets angry with you for something, she will manage her anger the way you've shown her anger should be managed—and treat you accordingly.

Q**uick Tip:** Do not ask your child to reveal the whereabouts of possessions that you are looking to retrieve from the co-parent's house.

What to Do When Your Co-Parent Bad-Mouths You

When the other parent is the one bad-mouthing you, resist fighting fire with fire. If you believe that modeling anger and hatred is damaging to your child, it stands to reason that you would not want the child to be exposed to double the amount of anger and hatred.

Q**uick Tip:** If your child asks you questions about the co-parent's life or about the specifics of your divorce, just say, "That's grown-up talk. That's not something we can discuss."

The rest of the advice on this topic is simple. If your child reports to you that the other parent has said something nasty about you, simply reply that you do not know why they would say that. Here are some examples:

Child: Mommy says that you love your new baby more than you love me.
Dad: I don't know why Mom would say that. I love you more than anything else in the whole world, and I always will.
Child: Daddy says that your boyfriend is a liar and a criminal.
Mom: I don't know why Daddy would say that. Maybe he was a little grumpy that day.

Your manner of reacting to what your child says will be just as important as the words you speak in response. If you speak the words with a purple face and clenched teeth, you will not be communicating the nonchalance that is important to reduce whatever concern the criticism has raised in your child.

Parents bad-mouth the other parent to the child to create doubt and insecurity in the child's mind. This is why it is such an unhealthy and damaging behavior. Your task in dealing with a bad-mouthing parent is to restore that security, not to prove your case to your child or get even with the other parent.

Resist the temptation to provide long-winded explanations to the child to disprove what the other parent has said. This draws the child right into the middle of your conflict with the co-parent, especially with children who feel the need to report your retort back to the co-parent.

As with many options for reducing co-parenting conflicts, taking the high road is a win-win situation. Save yourself the effort of generating detailed explanations about why the other parent was wrong and counterpoints of equally damaging information, and spend that energy showing your child your love. Even when children are swayed by a bad-mouthing co-parent, showing prudence in how you respond is always best. It is never wise to fight fire with fire.

When Bad-Mouthing Damages Your Relationship with Your Child

There are times when bad-mouthing parents do succeed in destroying a child's relationship with another parent. Many courts are very sympathetic to parents who can prove that another parent is teaching a child to be hateful and critical, but the process of educating decision makers still has a long way to go. If it appears as though you have tried to remove yourself from the conflict and have avoided using the same tactics, and this has not brought an end to the damage being done to the child, you must carefully document your child's behavior and consult an attorney so that you may seek court intervention. There is no certainty that court intervention will reverse the process, but at that point you will probably have to move ahead within the legal system in order to address the problem.

When Children Reject Their Parents

With ever-increasing frequency, children are reporting that they want nothing to do with one of their parents. I have spent the majority of my career studying visitation refusal and what others have called *parent alienation syndrome*. Personally, I do not favor the use of this term, primarily because the American Psychological Association does not recognize the phenomenon as a "syndrome," so if a psychologist uses this term in the context of a legal dispute, it is easily attacked because there is no reliable diagnostic category associated with it. Second, the term describes only half of the reason why children reject their parents, and it implies that the rejected parent is a passive victim whose child's mind was bent and twisted by the alienating parent. Most professionals, even professionals who favor use of the term *parental alienation*, acknowledge that the rejected parent usually contributes to the rejection by making such mistakes as becoming angry at the child, rejecting the child, and displaying anger at the other parent.

How the phenomenon of children rejecting their parents occurs is a matter of speculation and concern among mental health professionals; the fact that it does occur is indisputable. The degree to which the conflict of not wanting to see a parent affects a child's mental health is profound. It is profound enough to drive a child to self-destructive behavior.

If a child is forced against his will, he might run away or threaten to harm himself. While I have never seen a child harm himself over being forced to see a parent, I have been involved in cases where children have threatened it, and that is scary enough. I have also had the unfortunate experience of being involved in a case in which a child's guilt over rejecting a parent became so overwhelming that she took her own life.

Over the past ten years my staff and I have delivered more than ten thousand hours of reconciliation counseling in cases where children have refused to see their parents or have said they never want to see a parent again. The cases are not considered reconciliation counseling when they involve an act of physical abuse or neglect. These are cases where a child decides they no longer want to see a parent.

Often the precipitating event for cases like these is a child acting out the custodial parent's agenda. I have had children refuse to see a parent because there has not been enough child support paid. I have witnessed visitation being refused because children do not want to see or deal with a parent who has been unfaithful to the preferred or favored parent. At my clinic we have had children refuse visitation claiming the rejected parent is "not a nice person." The good news is that the vast majority of these cases end successfully, which is to say that the rejected parent and the child do reestablish a relationship with one another. The bad news is that the mental health community often hampers good results by promoting suggestions that are made with the best intentions but nevertheless prevent reconciliation. These suggestions include giving a child a rest or break from visitation, or suggesting the child not visit at all.

Don't Wait—Act Now

In my experience, the biggest mistake that people make when a parent is rejected is to wait for children "to come around." People mistakenly assume that if time goes by, children will forgive and forget. While this might happen in a percentage of cases, it is a very small percentage. Instead, children start to feel guilty about not visiting a parent. They worry that they will be scolded or made to feel bad that they didn't visit. Even young children know that they are disappointing and upsetting a parent they refuse to see. These bad feelings increase the child's motivation to avoid visitation, because they assume that the visit will be unpleasant or, at best, uncomfortable.

Children know that when they are not getting along well with a parent, the most anyone will force them to visit is once a week, so if they can convince the preferred parent to let them off the hook, they will not have to deal with the issue for a week. For most children, a week's reprieve from not having to face an uncomfortable circumstance is like being able to skip homework for a week and not get in trouble for it. There is generally no consequence to a child skipping visitation, because people can see that they are emotionally upset. It's natural to want to alleviate our children's emotional pain, so we are more likely to give in to children's requests for "a little more time" to forgive Mom or Dad.

As more time goes by, children have to become more creative with the excuses they give for not wanting to go on a visit, and as a result, emotions in the child run hotter, refusals become stronger, and the child becomes more upset, thus protesting more than ever against seeing the rejected parent. To make matters worse, while all of this is going on, Mom is blaming Dad for the lapse in visitation while Dad is blaming Mom; and this conflict is usually very obvious to the child, who in a very unhealthy way sees how the adults around him are so powerfully affected by his behavior.

Watching this sequence of events happen thousands of times has convinced me that when children and parents have lapses in their relationships, it is imperative that the child *not* be permitted to refuse to visit, and that both parents should make efforts to get that child into counseling with a therapist who understands the phenomenon and how to deal with it.

Unfortunately, most therapists do not know how to deal with it, and, after a few weak attempts at trying to restructure the relationship, conclude that it's best not to force visitation but instead to wait until the child gets older and comes looking for a relationship. This reasoning makes sense to a lot of people, but it does not make sense to me. We do not permit a child to stay home from school simply because she doesn't want to go. We do not permit a child to refuse to go to the doctor when he needs medical treatment. We do not permit a child to go to bed without brushing her teeth simply because the child "doesn't like the way it feels."

Yet, we *are*, in case after case of visitation refusal, allowing children to "divorce" a parent simply because it does not "feel right." Perhaps it is too difficult to believe that children can reject a parent forever. Perhaps it is because we believe that if a child does not want to see a parent, it must be for a good reason.

More likely, it is because children see the two most important people in their lives hate each other, abandon each other, and proclaim how much better life is when we rid ourselves of the people who made us so unhappy. Children from high-conflict divorce see poor interpersonal problem solving, poor conflict resolution, motivation for revenge, disrespect, antagonism, even violence. Why would it be so unusual for children to compartmentalize all of the anger they have over the breakup of their family and merely eliminate half the source of their disappointment? As I mentioned in the previous section, parents who permit their children to reject the other parent should prepare to receive the same treatment themselves.

When you teach a child to hate, you cannot control who the targets of that hatred ultimately become. Sometimes, in the most distressing of all outcomes, we find that children whose hatred and rage originate in family conflict go outside of their families, to their schoolmates and to strangers, to act it out, the results of which are ultimately communicated in the news media.

Topic 48
What to Do When Your Child Is Acting Out Sexually During or After a Visit

MANY PARENTS' BIGGEST nightmare is that their child might be sexually abused. In a high proportion of sexual molestations cases, the perpetrator is close to the family. What should you do if your child does something that appears very sexual, and you believe that the child might have been exposed to sexual activity at the co-parent's house?

Children can learn sexual behavior by being the recipient of it, by observing and imitating it, or by exploring their own bodies and experiencing the pleasurable sensations that occur while doing so. The last circumstance is normal, natural, and not harmful. The first two circumstances are harmful to children to varying degrees, depending on what they have been exposed to.

Educating Your Child

Every parent, from the time a child is about three years of age or so, can and should start to educate their child about sexual behavior by explaining the names of the private areas of the body and by explaining the difference between good touches—like hugs and back scratches given by people you know very well—and bad touches, which are any touches that make you feel uncomfortable or creepy, and particularly any touches in the private areas.

It is often helpful to give children age five and above very specific advice about how people can touch or kiss them. This includes teaching children to give and receive kisses on the cheek and to tell an adult when someone tries to kiss them on the mouth. Giving a child a kiss on the lips is acceptable in some cultures, but I would rather have a child offend some of my Old World family members and be certain the child knows the difference between an appropriate versus an inappropriate form of affection. Besides, it is not the most sanitary way of interacting with a child, and for this reason alone you should teach your child to avoid it.

Children can learn a lot of age-inappropriate sexual behavior by watching television. A rash of parents have come through my office whose children have seen people kissing with their tongues on television and who then imitate the behavior. Of course, this can become the catalyst for horrible fights and accusations between co-parents. It is always wise to monitor and restrict television for children. Children can watch television, but television should not watch children.

When to Get a Professional Opinion

If your child demonstrates any of the following behaviors, a safe course of action is to discuss it immediately with a pediatrician or child behavior expert.

- Tries to kiss on the mouth and spontaneously says that is the way so-and-so kisses
- Compulsively masturbates
- Tries to insert objects into body openings
- Is involved in sexual behavior (oral sex, simulated or actual intercourse) with playmates
- Makes sexually explicit comments without knowing their meaning
- Makes sexual advances to other adults (touches or rubs or tries to kiss their genitals)

The physical signs of sex abuse are difficult for the untrained eye to identify accurately. Children may be prone to rashes and irritations in the genital area that can be related to acidic urine, as well as certain soaps or laundry detergents. Before accusing anyone of sexual impropriety with your child, get a professional opinion.

If Sexual Abuse Is Confirmed

When indications appear to confirm your suspicions that your child might have been exposed to sexual activity, you must talk with the co-parent and share your concerns. You can do so without pointing an accusatory finger, but there is no guarantee that it will be taken as anything other than accusatory. Do not take this as a sign of guilt or culpability on the part of the person you are talking to. While it is frightening to think your child might be sexually abused, it is also frightening to be unjustly accused of sexually abusing your own child.

Both parents must put their heads together to discuss who the child has been interacting with lately and any other pertinent observations. Both parents should meet with professionals trained in this area and seek their advice.

All cases of suspected sexual abuse should be reported to whatever child protective service agency handles your jurisdiction. The telephone number for this agency is usually found at the beginning or end of the local telephone directory. You can also get this number from directory assistance by asking for the listing for the government agency in your area that handles cases of suspected child abuse. A child who reports abuse by a parent is somewhat at the mercy of the professionals who examine that child and the opinions they form as a result of examining the child. Be certain, therefore, that the people who examine your children have the requisite training and skill.

The quality of service received from any government employee who investigates child or sexual abuse varies from excellent to poor, depending on the training of the individual, experience in the field, and many other factors. You have the right to ask workers questions about their training. Take careful notes about everything an investigator does with respect to places, times, and contact with the child.

If you believe that a caseworker did not do an adequate job of investigating the abuse, find out who supervises that worker and ask whether you may submit a letter reflecting your concerns. If you believe you have been unjustly accused, you should seek a lawyer's advice. In most jurisdictions there is a protocol for challenging the investigative findings of a state agency that handles child abuse.

If you are very sure that your child has been sexually molested by the co-parent or someone at the co-parent's house, before you cancel the next visitation, speak to an attorney or go to court and ask about how you can file for an emergency action or conference with the court on your child's behalf.

This is a very difficult parenting area because children can be swayed to report sex abuse that did not happen, and they can be convinced or threatened not to report abuse that did happen. You can protect your children's interests by supervising them closely at all times. Teach your children to talk about their bodies, to not be ashamed of any body part, to be cautious of anyone who touches their bodies or makes them feel uncomfortable, and to always tell an adult when this happens.

Topic 49
What to Do When Your Child Tells You He or She Was Hit at the Co-Parent's House

THERE IS A difference between being spanked and being hit. Neither spanking nor hitting a child is a particularly good way of changing behavior. Aggressive discipline creates aggressive children, whether the physical contact is not considered abuse but "acceptable corporal punishment" (usually a swat on the backside with your open hand or a slap on the wrist), or whether it is considered abuse (striking a child hard enough to leave a mark, striking a child in the face or head area, striking a child with an object like a belt or shoe). Not all states have the same definition of abuse, so if you do use corporal punishment on your children, you had better be aware of what is considered criminal or neglectful and what is considered acceptable.

Your child may come home to you or may come to visitation complaining of being physically disciplined by the other parent. If that happens, you can either immediately accuse the other parent of being a child abuser and set out to prove it to the world, or you can rationally investigate to see whether your child is in danger.

As with many other topics I have discussed in this book, you can ask a co-parent a nonthreatening question, but it will not always be taken as such. That should not stop you from asking your question in a neutral and civilized way, regardless of what you suspect the reaction will be. This is one of many appropriate ways to begin such a conversation with the co-parent: "Billy came to my house a little cranky today. Is there anything that you know of that is bothering him?"

This might be the start of a productive discussion, or it might be a replay of other arguments that ultimately have an unproductive ending. If it does not turn into an immediate argument, you can continue by saying: "One of the things that he mentioned while he was talking was that he got spanked and it hurt him. Did you spank him today for something?" This statement is a lot more straightforward than the first statement, but it is still very appropriate, and it is merely reporting information. As always, this is not to suggest you will get a pleasant reaction.

You can soften that by saying, "I did not call to argue or criticize, and I know that Billy can be a handful, but maybe there is a different way of handling him when he misbehaves." If you are able to get this far, at the very least you will have communicated your concerns. In a high-conflict, poor co-parenting relationship, this is about as far as you will get in most cases.

> **Q**uick **Tip:** Do ask your child questions about where he got a suspicious-looking welt or bruise. If the child says he was hit, call your co-parent to see what went on, and then call child welfare authorities if you think there was abuse.

Determining Whether Your Child Is in Danger

You must now decide whether your child's complaints represent a danger to him. Pay attention to the following cues:

- You notice marks or bruises on fleshy parts of the arms, thighs, and buttocks—especially those that look like four dots or finger marks close together—or two parallel lines or half-moon marks that can be from pinching. Belt marks look like slashes on the back, buttocks, or backs of thighs. Accidental bruising from play or clumsiness usually occurs on bony prominences such as chins, shins, foreheads, and elbows. While there is no way of generalizing, you can use these descriptions as very broad guidelines.

- Your child is afraid or emotional when she tells the story of what happened.
- Reports of suspected abuse come to you from teachers or from other people in your child's life who may be responsible for reporting physical abuse.
- Your child displays increased aggressiveness.
- You notice flinching when you move near your child or try to play or roughhouse in a normal way.

If communicating with the co-parent is impossible, and your child is saying that he is hit or hurt at the other parent's house, the suggested course of action is as follows.

- Take your child to the pediatrician for an examination of any suspicious marks or bruises. If you cannot contact the pediatrician, take your child to the local emergency room. Pediatricians and emergency room doctors are required by law to report suspected abuse or neglect.
- Make an appointment for your child to be interviewed by a behavioral counselor who is familiar with the signs and symptoms of physical abuse.
- Consult an attorney on the correct procedure to protect your child by court intervention.

If you decide to restrict visitation on the basis of what your child tells you, do so cautiously, and be certain that you have had input from treating professionals and from your attorney about whether this is advisable.

Part 8
Moving On

Topic 50
Introducing Your Child to Your New Partner

THE ADVICE IN this section will be very difficult for most of you to agree with. That being said, let me also say that generalizing about people whose lives may be very complicated is difficult to do, so these are just general guidelines not informed by your particular story.

My rule of thumb is that divorced parents should keep children out of their social lives until they have been separated or divorced for a period of *at least two years* and you have known your potential new partner for *at least a year*. Let me explain the easy things first.

Quick **Tip:** When it comes to introducing your kids to the people you are dating, wait, wait, wait. Then think it through, wait some more, and start talking about the person who is becoming special and whom you would like them to meet. Even when you are careful as can be, children might not warm up to the idea of your dating for a long time. One thing is certain—if you rush it, there will be problems.

Extramarital Affairs

It is definitely not a good idea to include your children as participants in social outings with someone you are having an extramarital affair with. This places your children in a very uncomfortable circumstance, and some judges consider this a very egregious example of poor parenting judgment, which might ultimately result in your losing custody of the children. It doesn't matter if "the marriage was over a long time ago" in the figurative sense, either.

Quick Tip: Never, ever bring your children around a partner or lover while you are still married. It might seem overly
strict, but it can save you lots of stress in the end.

Your children might still consider you and your soon-to-be-ex a family, and they may they feel uncomfortable or betrayed by your including
them in activities with your boyfriend or girlfriend.

I once worked on a case in which a mother was locking herself in
the bedroom and talking for hours via computer with the person she
was having an affair with. Because she was not very computer literate,
she would ask her son to help her get online. Later this child found out
(through the equally poor judgment of his father) that the mother was
conducting an online romance. The child believed he somehow participated in the breakup of the marriage because he unwittingly "helped"
her talk to her boyfriend. This mother never understood why her son
could not adjust to the boyfriend's presence in the house later on.

Do not bring your children into your extramarital relationships.
Also, even if it is true (and it rarely is true), no one will believe that
the person whose children had playdates with your children, who you
wound up having an affair with, was not your boyfriend or girlfriend
the whole while.

In the worst of all circumstances, your children are enlisted as
"spies" by the parent who suspects the affair and are interrogated mer-
cilessly, or they become "secret agents" who are sworn to secrecy about
their parents' affairs. Don't do this to your children; they have enough
to worry about.

New Partners

You might think your new partner is the greatest thing since sliced
bread, but at one time you thought the same thing about the person
whose name is on the bottom of the restraining order you just got. It's
hard to resist the power of someone who not only makes you feel good
about yourself but reinforces your negative feelings about your ex.

With all of that conflict to concentrate on (especially if *both* of you are going through divorces), who has time to create trouble in the new relationship? What happens as a result is an extended "honeymoon period" in the new relationship. Having your kids along with your new partner helps legitimize the relationship, especially if your kids like your new partner's kids and everyone gets along—but it might very well place unnecessary pressure on the kids.

When Your Children Call Your New Partner Mom or Dad

Your kids might like your partner so much they call him or her a variation of Mom or Dad, which is great if the person treats the children like his or her own, and if your children have no real mommy or daddy who will take you to court for trying to interfere with their parental relationship.

In most instances it is simply not a good idea to encourage the children to refer to another parent figure as Mom or Dad when they already have a mother or father in their lives. On occasion, when parents are more emotionally well adjusted than I could ever be, there is no objection to a child referring to two parent figures as Mom or Dad. When this is the case, and everyone is happy, it is fine. If you *know* you will resent someone else being called Mom or Dad, do not agree to it.

Reasons to Take It Slow

One reason to take it very slow in having your children cozy up to your new partner is that often, the "second time around" relationship is just as bad as or worse than the first relationship you had, and you want to get away from that person too. That may be fine for you, but what if your kids like that person and the people who tag along with him or her? What happens then is that your children go through another round of sad separations, and ultimately they become mistrustful and suspicious of the next round of people you bring them into contact with. For kids, these separations can be as painful as the divorce from their mother or father.

Then there are the situations where you bring your children into contact with your new partner and they *hate* that person. What you have created in that circumstance is a pipeline of complaints that go from your children to the other parent, and that creates yet another set of problems.

Quick Tip: Split loyalties are common when children are brought into a relationship with a parent's new partner. It will take patience and an ability to be warm, but stay in the background to get past this.

Children of divorced parents often feel split loyalties between a new partner or parent figure and a biological parent. This is made worse when one of the biological parents is insecure or angry. It is very easy for children to pick up on, and as a result they try to please and soothe that parent by being critical of Mom or Dad's new boyfriend or girlfriend.

With all of the problems that are associated with bringing children into contact with new boyfriends and girlfriends, it is a wonder why people do it with such frequency. There are two main reasons: One is that when parents separate they yearn for the return of a "normal" life with a companion. In their desire to create that normal life, they make decisions too quickly or without thinking through all of the possibilities and often end up replacing one dysfunctional relationship with another. As adults we are entitled to do this until we get it right, but we should try to avoid exposing children to our dating disasters. Related to this is the second main reason—when a parent adopts the philosophy that "My kids and I come as a package deal. If you think you want to be with me, my kids have to approve." This is a perfectly reasonable philosophy, but it must be employed later rather than sooner. You should figure out whether the person is worth having your children evaluate them first.

Why the Two-Year Rule Works

I advocate the two-year rule because by the one-year mark most couples have seen each other at their best and at their worst. If you have seen your partner at your worst and he or she does not try to damage your self-esteem when you fight, and you have successfully solved many of the relationship problems you could not solve with your ex, then your relationship has a better than 50-50 chance of succeeding in the long term. I have seen quite a few complicated and difficult circumstances arise because people are in too much of a hurry to introduce their children to their new partners.

Another advantage is that after some time has passed, even young children will expect their mothers and fathers to want companionship, and the children will not be as focused on wanting to reunite the family. There is no guarantee your child will ever stop wanting this, but in most cases children will want it less after a few years or at least accept the reality that it's not going to happen.

Once you have passed the two-year mark of being out of your old relationship, and once you know your new partner for a year, you can start talking to your children about meeting your boyfriend or girlfriend. If your children are old enough to understand what a boyfriend or girlfriend is, don't beat around the bush. This is actually one of the advantages you have gained by waiting such a long time before introducing the person.

The Sleepover Question

Different people have different ideas about whether parents should invite their boyfriends or girlfriends to sleep over at their house. I would say avoid it, especially with young children. Children are growing up very quickly these days, and they will start to ask questions about whether you are having sex with your boyfriend or girlfriend because you are sleeping with them. You could properly tell them this is none of their business, but the situation will nevertheless make them feel uncomfortable, and you will ultimately have to deal with what kind of model this presents to your children, especially when they are fifteen years old and want to bring their boyfriends and girlfriends home to your house to sleep over.

Finally, it might be very tempting to bring your little children into bed with you and your new partner to snuggle or watch television, but I have seen this cause problems between moms and dads who become furious at the thought of their children climbing into bed with someone who is a "stranger" to them and cuddling. Before you permit your child to do this, ask yourself it is worth the legal fees you will have to spend in order to convince someone that you think there is no harm in it.

Topic 51
Stepparenting

THE ROLE OF a stepparent in a stepchild's life can be very different depending on what circumstances surround the relationship between stepparent and stepchild.

If You or Your Co-Parent Is Not Remarried but a New Partner Is Involved

If you and your new partner are not married, there is no stepparent relationship between your partner and your children, and that means you should never let that partner assume he or she should have any say in how or when children are disciplined. You can try to make the case that your new partner is an older person to your children and therefore should be respected—and of course this is true. Children should respect adults, but a stepparent is a very special type of adult—one who is related to you, the biological parent.

> **Q**uick Tip: Unless the biological parent is completely out of the picture from a very young age, boyfriends and girlfriends who are not stepparents (and even, to some extent, stepparents) should always play a much lesser role in disciplining children.

Let's say you are the biological mother of a child and you are living with someone, and your child says something very disrespectful to you. If your boyfriend steps in and sends your child to her room, it is a very bad move. You are the one who should be disciplining in this situation. Your boyfriend can be as offended as anyone in this circumstance would be, but he should not step in or hand out punishments and should never, ever spank or hit your child. In nonmarital arrangements, the biological parent needs to be the disciplinarian.

' Whether you are a mother or a father, you always want to control for the possibility that your current arrangement might ultimately not work out. If you permit your partner to walk away from the relationship being the one who disciplines the children, you might have a very difficult time establishing yourself as the primary person of influence over the children.

Similarly, if your partner turns out to be a bad person, and your children knew it all the while, if you had given that person too much power in your household you might see your children upset at you for not ending your relationship sooner or exposing the children to someone they might not have liked in the first instance.

If You or Your Co-Parent Is Remarried

In the case of remarriage, is the child required to listen to and mind the stepparent as a biological parent? That depends on a lot of factors, but generally speaking the stepparent should play a secondary role in matters of discipline and influence, even if you are convinced that he or she is a better parent to your child than the biological parent.

If your child has little or no access to his other "real" parent, and the stepparent is the only parent the child has ever known, this doesn't necessarily make life any easier for you or the stepparent. It can be just as difficult for the stepparent to compete with the idealized parent your child imagines his other biological parent to be. In short, there is almost no situation that will prevent your child from firing the phrase "I don't have to listen to you—you're not my mother [father]" to his stepparent.

Between the totally absent biological parent and the totally present biological parent are a lot of different configurations. Life is always better when everyone can get along. When stepmother and biological mother have an understanding with one another, and when stepfather and biological father have an understanding, those are good situations. When there is competition, hatred and loyalty issues can get significantly more complicated. When that happens, the stepparent should default to being a background influence on the child.

Topic 52
Your New Beginning

IT'S TIME THAT you let there be a new beginning. Divorce is traumatic, life changing, complicated, and emotional—but the divorce process should have a beginning, a middle, and an end. You must sometimes work very hard to reach a point where your divorce and your problems with the co-parent are somewhere in the "less important" categories of your life—but it is essential to your mental health that you let yourself get there.

Part of the difficulty that people have in post-divorce life is the issue of closure and the confusing emotions that the end of relationships sometimes bring about—you want to end the relationship, but you don't want to let it go. This is difficult even in relationships where there are no children involved. But it can be more difficult when the marriage produced children; many parents see each other in the behavior, mannerisms, and physical appearance of their children, and this can make a clean break that much more difficult.

You and your co-parent will always be involved with one another, because even after children grow up they still get married, have children, and perpetuate the circle of life, all of which require the participation of you and your co-parent.

The best part about all of this is that the older children get, the better they are at understanding what each of their parents is dealing with. You children will never be too old for you to show them the value of tolerance, taking the high road, and civilized control of one's emotions. As children get older it becomes easier to appreciate the contributions of the parent who fusses less, bends more, and refuses to sour at the thought of having to occupy the same space as the co-parent.

Do yourself a favor and start earning that appreciation sooner rather than later!

Resources

The Uniform Child Custody Jurisdiction Act (UCCJA)
law.upenn.edu/bll/ulc/fnact99/1920-69/uccja68.htm
Overview of the Uniform Child Custody Jurisdiction Act

Custody
custodysource.com
An enormous state-by-state directory of custody resources

divorcesource.com
Another comprehensive list of resources for custody and divorce

afccnet.org
Association of Family and Conciliation Courts

Child Sexual Abuse

darkness2light.org/GetHelp/national.asp
List of national resources for child abuse

jccany.org/site/PageServer?pagename=resources_caa_one
List of symptoms related to child physical and sexual abuse

Substance Abuse

ncadi.samhsa.gov
Drug and alcohol abuse information from the U.S. Department
   of Health and Human Services Substance Abuse and Mental
   Health Services Administration

aa.org
Home page of Alcoholics Anonymous

Domestic Violence

abanet.org/domviol/home.html
The American Bar Association Commission on Domestic
   Violence

atask.org
Asian Task Force Against Domestic Violence

cavnet.org
Communities Against Violence Network (CAVNET)

faithtrustinstitute.org
Center for the Prevention of Sexual and Domestic Violence

HELPUSA.org
National domestic violence assistance

childadvocates.org
Domestic violence as it pertains to kids

fvpf.org
Family Violence Prevention Fund

growing.com/nonviolent
Domestic Violence Project of Silicon Valley

hawc.org
Houston Area Women's Center

www.biscmi.org
Batterer Intervention Services Coalition

members.tripod.com/elkcountycapsea
CAPSEA, Inc. (Citizens Against Physical, Sexual, and Emotional
Abuse)

ncdsv.org/publications_childsupportcustody.html
Resource Center on Domestic Violence: Child Protection and
Custody

ncjrs.org
National Criminal Justice Reference Service

ndvh.org
National Domestic Violence Hotline (1-800-799-SAFE
[7233]; 1-800-787-3224 [TDD])

nyawc.org
New York Asian Women's Center (NYAWC)

opdv.state.ny.us
New York State Office for the Prevention of Domestic Violence
(OPDV)

ovw.usdoj.gov
United States Department of Justice Office on Violence Against Women

cted.wa.gov/portal/alias-CTED//ang-en/tabID-244/Desktop Default.aspx
The Office of Crime Victims Advocacy, a Washington state agency, and the Washington State Department of Social and Health Services have developed a website for domestic and sexual assault service providers in Washington.

Index

306.89
F272

LINCOLN CHRISTIAN UNIVERSITY

121738

3 4711 00200 0380